AP® U.S. Government and Politics

EXPRESS

KAPLAN

PUBLISHING

New York

AP® is a registered trademark of the College Board, which neither sponsors nor endorses this product. This publication is designed to provide accurate and authoritative information in regard to the subject matter covered. It is sold with the understanding that the publisher is not engaged in rendering legal, accounting, or other professional service. If legal advice or other expert assistance is required, the services of a competent professional should be sought.

© 2010 by Kaplan, Inc.

Published by Kaplan Publishing, a division of Kaplan, Inc.
395 Hudson Street
New York, NY 10014

Printed in the United States of America

10 9 8 7 6 5 4 3 2 1

ISBN 978-1-60714-788-6

Kaplan Publishing books are available at special quantity discounts to use for sales promotions, employee premiums, or educational purposes. For more information or to purchase books, please call the Simon & Schuster special sales department at 866-506-1949.

Table of Contents

How to Take the Test

ABOUT THIS BOOK

If you are taking an AP U.S. Government and Politics course at your high school, or if you have a good foundation in U.S. government and politics and strong composition skills, taking the exam can help you earn college credit and placement into advanced coursework. Think of the money and time you can save! It can also improve your chances of acceptance to competitive schools, because colleges know that AP students are better prepared for college.

In the following pages, you will find information about the format of the exam, test-taking strategies, and an extensive review of essential topics that will help you to identify your strengths and weaknesses, and establish a study plan.

The first thing you need to do is find out what is on the AP U.S. Government and Politics exam. The next section presents the overall test structure and a brief overview of its scoring. You'll find background information about the test and the most effective strategies to help you score your best, including guidelines for successful multiple-choice testing and essay construction.

With Kaplan's proven test-taking strategies, dozens of practice questions, an extensive review of key topics, and guidelines for writing your essay responses, you will be able to take the exam with confidence.

> **AP EXPERT TIP**
>
> Try to allow yourself at least 30 minutes nightly to review. Use this guide along with your textbook, class handouts, and Internet resources for content mastery.

ABOUT THE TEST

The AP U.S. Government and Politics exam is 2 hours and 25 minutes long. You will have 45 minutes to complete the first section, which consists of 60 multiple choice questions. You will have 1 hour and 40 minutes to complete the second section, which consists of 4 free-response, or essay, questions.

Section I: Multiple-choice	60 questions	45 minutes	50% of the exam
Section II: Essays	4 questions	100 minutes	50% of the exam

The exam covers the various institutions, groups, beliefs, and principles that make-up U.S. government and politics. Questions on the AP U.S. Government and Politics exam reflect the following six major content areas:

I. **Institutions of National Government: the Congress, the Presidency, the Bureaucracy, and the Federal Courts** (35%–45%)

    (organization and powers; relationships between these institutions and public opinion and voters; interest groups; political parties; the media; and state and local governments)

II. **Political Beliefs and Behaviors** (10%–20%)

(factors that influence political beliefs and behaviors; nature, sources and consequences of public opinion, voting patterns and participation)

III. **Political Parties, Interest Groups, and Mass Media** (10%–20%)

(functions, structures, development, and impacts of each)

IV. **Constitutional Underpinnings of United States Government** (5%–15%)

(federalism, separation of powers, checks and balances)

V. **Public Policy** (5%–15%)

(creation and enactment of public policies by Congress and the president; execution and interpretation of policies by the bureaucracy and courts)

VI. **Civil Rights and Civil Liberties** (5%–15%)

(analysis of significant Supreme Court decisions; judicial interpretations of freedom of speech, assembly, expression; the rights of the accused; the rights of minority groups and women)

The multiple-choice section of the exam is dedicated to each content area in the approximate percentages listed. The essay section of the exam will test you in some combination of these topics. Use these topics as a guideline to help you focus your study.

❯❯ WHAT THE TEST REQUIRES

Although the AP U.S. Government and Politics exam is not a test that one passes or fails, generally a 3 or higher on the 5-point scale is necessary to receive advanced placement, credit, or both from the college of your choice.

The best way to find out what the test requires is to look at the practice sections in this book. They include detailed explanations for the answers to each muliple-choice question. Practice your responses to the essay questions. Use the scoring guides provided to get a sense of your own strengths and weaknesses.

The AP U.S. Government and Politics exam tests your analytical skills and factual knowledge. The multiple-choice and essay questions require you to know key facts, concepts, and theories pertaining to U.S. government and politics. However, the exam does not test your knowledge of specific dates. You will also be asked to interpret basic data, analyze and apply relevant theories, establish connections, and draw meaningful conclusions.

❯❯ HOW THE TEST IS SCORED

The multiple-choice section makes up half of your score. Your score for the multiple-choice section is based on the total number of correct answers. No points are deducted for wrong answers. The essay section makes up the other half of your score. Your essays are read and graded by trained AP teachers and college faculty. These two scores are combined to give a composite score, which is converted to the AP's 5-point scale.

> ❯ **AP EXPERT TIP**
>
> Many states, such as Minnesota, Texas, and Wisconsin, post online or offer in hard copy the AP test score requirements for the various colleges and universities within the state. These will vary from state to state, just as score requirements vary from college to college.

All AP exams are rated on a scale of 1 to 5, with 5 as the highest:

5 Extremely well qualified

4 Well qualified

3 Qualified

2 Possibly qualified

1 No recommendation

For more information about the AP U.S. Government and Politics exam and other AP exams, check the College Board AP website at **apcentral.collegeboard.com**.

❯❯ HOW TO APPROACH THE MULTIPLE-CHOICE SECTION

Here are some tips for doing well on the multiple-choice section of the test:

Answer in Your Own Order

Rather than taking the test in a completely linear way, use these steps:

1. Answer all the questions that you know and are sure about first.

2. Go through the questions you were not sure about and mark them based on your familiarity with the topic.
   - If the topic is familiar and you can eliminate at least two answer choices, mark the question by **circling** the question number, and move on.
   - If you do *not* remember the topic, mark the question with an **X**, and move on.

3. Go back through the test and answer the questions circled. Try to eliminate at least three choices, then take your best guess.

4. Go back and answer the questions you marked with an X. Again, try to eliminate at least two or three choices, and take an educated guess.

Read Actively

The main part of a test question, before the answer choices, is called the *stem*. Read the question stem carefully, paying particular attention to key words such as *only, except, always, not, never,* and *best.* Underline key words and phrases in the question.

Predict an Answer

Before you look at the answer choices, try to think of the answer on your own. This will help you narrow the choices and avoid being seduced by wrong answers that *seem* right at first glance. Wrong answer choices are also known as *distracters* because they *distract* you from the right answer.

Use the Process of Elimination

As you read through the possible responses, cross off the ones you know are wrong. Be sure to read every possible answer before you make your selection. When eliminating distracters, think about whether each choice is outside of the time period or category of the question.

Pace Yourself

You have 45 minutes to complete 60 questions. Move quickly but thoroughly through the test. Do not linger on any single question for more than about 30 seconds. Check to make sure you have gridded in all responses correctly.

Remember, every correct answer adds to your score, and there is no penalty for incorrect answers. **So be sure to answer every question!**

Practice multiple-choice questions, with detailed answer explanations, are provided at the ends of chapters 1 and 4.

❯❯ HOW TO APPROACH THE ESSAY QUESTIONS

The second part of the AP U.S. Government and Politics exam is the essay section. This section inspires the most dread in the minds of students taking the test. However, understanding the structure, timing, and scoring of the essays can give you a big advantage. Here are some tips for doing well on the essay section of the test:

Answer in Your Own Order

You do not have to answer the essays in the order in which they appear. When you open your essay test packet, scan all the questions and choose the essay for which you have the most ready response. Beginning with your strongest area will help boost your confidence.

Read Critically

Before you start writing, read and decode each essay prompt carefully. What is it asking? Is there more than one part to the question? Read the prompt with your pen in your hand. Underline, circle, and make notations.

Organize and Structure Your Essay

For each type of essay question, be sure to:

- discuss the thesis or position
- use specific examples to support that position
- answer all parts of the question
- analyze and describe—don't retell
- stick to the topic at hand

Don't include personal opinions in the essay. The reader is looking for your grasp of the material itself and your ability to write about it. Discuss each topic given. Giving information on other topics will not win you any points.

A longer essay is not necessarily better, but it takes more than a paragraph or two to merit a good score. As a general rule, aim for five parts: an introduction, three body paragraphs, and a conclusion. Another good rule of thumb is one body paragraph for each portion of the essay prompt.

Write It Out

Write as neatly and as legibly as you can. Test scorers understand that your essays are drafts. Cross-outs, inserted lines with arrows, and other working thoughts are acceptable as long as they are clear. However, avoid using abbreviations, shorthand symbols (such as & or @) or texting spelling. If the reader does not understand the symbol or word, he or she will ignore it, and you might not gain a point.

You must write an *essay* for each question. Bullet notes, diagrams, or lists of information are not considered essay format and will be ignored by the reader.

Pace Yourself

A total of 100 minutes, or 1 hour and 40 minutes, is allotted for reading, organizing, and writing all four questions. Your proctor will *not* tell you to move from one essay to the next—you must do this on your own.

Each essay counts for one-fourth, or 25 percent, of your total essay grade. So you should spend one-fourth of your allotted time (25 minutes) on each essay. You do not want to rush through the essays too quickly, and you do not want to run out of time. Partial essays do not receive high scores. Bring a watch, and budget your time for each essay.

Practice free-response questions, with scoring guides for each question type, are provided at the ends of chapters 2 and 3.

▶ **AP EXPERT TIPS**

1. Remember techniques like Pacing, Process of Elimination, and Reading Critically.
2. Know how to manage your stress. You can beat anxiety the same way you can beat the exam—by knowing what to expect beforehand and developing strategies to deal with it.
3. Take Kaplan's practice tests to learn your test-taking strengths and weaknesses. Knowing these will allow you to focus on your problem areas as you prepare for test day.
4. Get organized! Make a study schedule between now and test day and give yourself plenty of time to prepare. Waiting until the last minute to cram info is not only unwise but exhausting.
5. Make a test day game plan. Have everything you need to bring to the exam ready the night before. Make it a priority to eat a good breakfast. Avoid overindulging in caffeine. Read something to warm up your brain. And finally, get to the test site early.

CHAPTER 1

Beginnings of Democratic Thought

❯❯ I. THE DEVELOPMENT OF THE U.S. FEDERAL SYSTEM

Steps from the Declaration of Independence to the Constitution

Thomas Jefferson and the committee of leaders of the Continental Congress agreed on a statement that explained the need for separation from the United Kingdom. The Declaration of Independence lists many abuses brought about by bad leadership, inspired by King George III. Using John Locke's "Second Treatise of Civil Government" as a model, Jefferson wrote that government exists to provide liberties and freedoms for those who agree to the rules and limits. He paraphrased the English philosopher John Locke's statement "life, liberty, and property" as "life, liberty, and the pursuit of happiness" to emphasize the fundamental goal of the country's governmental structure.

When the United States gained independence in 1781, a plan for rule—the Articles of Confederation—had already been debated and accepted. Drafted by a committee headed by John Dickinson, the Articles allowed for the dominance of local and state authority, control of taxes at the regional level, and a form of voluntary union by the states. This "free" government could not deal effectively with threats from foreign nations, disagreements between states, or resulting financial chaos. The Articles failed for the following reasons:

- No national executive branch was established.
- There was no separate judiciary.
- The central government could not collect taxes, but states were expected to volunteer extra funds—although the states were bankrupt.
- A unanimous vote of *all* states was needed to create any needed amendments, a challenging requirement because the states were constantly feuding.
- Major laws had to be approved by 9 of the 13 states, which made passing legislation very difficult.
- Congress did not have the power to regulate commerce, which caused serious tensions between states.

Many of the governmental items missing in the Articles of Confederation were added in the new document. Many who later objected to the Constitution made sure the basic freedoms listed in the Declaration of Independence were added in the form of a federal Bill of Rights.

The Difficult Convention

It is important to remember how difficult the creation of the Constitution turned out to be and how close the debates came to collapsing. Several important leaders, such as Patrick Henry, refused to participate. Rhode Island refused to allow any representatives to attend. Delaware threatened other states that it would not participate in a treasonous "coup." The New York delegation was so divided that all three members left in disgust and two (John Lansing and Robert Yates) would try to defeat the ratification effort. Governor Edmund Randolph of Virginia, a key state, refused to sign the document and also campaigned against it. Both New York's and Virginia's meetings would struggle for long periods before ratification.

FORMATION OF CONGRESS

The biggest challenge of the convention was the issue of representation in Congress. Under the Articles of Confederation, each state had an equal vote, no matter what its population. States with large populations were determined to have greater representation than those with smaller populations. But smaller states refused to create a system where they could be dominated by growing regions. The outcome of this power struggle became known as the "Great Compromise." According to this agreement, state representation in the House of Representatives would be based on population, while in the Senate each state was given an equal vote.

Another major issue at the convention was determining the appropriate balance of power between the national and state governments. Those who favored a strong central government and those who favored the political power of individual states were forerunners of the coming splits between Federalists and Anti-Federalists. This would be the central division between the first party leaders, Hamilton and Jefferson. The delegates also deadlocked on the issue of how to count slaves for the purpose of determining the number of representatives each state would have in the House of Representatives. The compromise reached was the horrible precedent of counting every five slaves as three free men.

Ratification Issues

Only with the inclusion of a federal Bill of Rights did the states agree to put the new Constitution into force. Approval from only 9 of the 13 existing states was required for ratification, and 9 states completed this by the summer of 1788. However, opponents held up the process in New York and Virginia. The nation understood that if either of these key states rejected the Constitution, the other nine votes would be meaningless. Proponents called for giving the new system a trial, knowing that time for discussion was being reduced by foreign threats.

During the months of state meetings concerning the possible adoption of the new Constitution, many essays were written in newspapers that defended or attacked the plan. The most famous essays were written by Madison and Hamilton and were later collected as a book under the title *Federalist Papers*. To attract some moderate or undecided leadership, the writers did not list their own names but collectively used "Publius," a reference to Roman debates about good government. The essays stand as great explanations of how the U.S. government balances power, protects different political factions, settles disputes, and runs the diverse nation. Madison's essay "Number 10" is regarded as a definitive essay about regional political divisions. He used the word *factions* to describe how local governments could not handle minorities without the dangers of abuse by local majorities. This essay also explains that "factions" should have greater national access, a prediction of lobby groups and early party organizations. Essay "Number 51, " probably written by Madison, is known as the great defense of the balance and separations of power within this new plan. Hamilton's "Number 78" provided the basis for the later development of the doctrine of judicial review.

Anti-Federalists had critical points to make about having a single executive leader, the excessive power to tax, and excessive federal power. Even though at that time, each state had a bill of rights in its state constitution, Anti-Federalists successfully forced Federalists to agree to add more definitions of rights as amendments. When the first Congress convened in 1789, Representative James Madison led the effort to create 12 proposals, and 10 were adopted as the new Bill of Rights.

The Development of Parties Under the Constitution

Most sources agree that the early federal republic also saw the creation of political parties under the leadership of Hamilton and Jefferson:

Federalists held views similar to those of Tories in the English government. They wanted a strong central government, especially economically and militarily. They were reacting to the memories of the chaos of the English Civil War and the weak central government under the Articles of Confederation.

Democratic-Republicans supported states' rights and held that tolerance, freedoms, and independent actions were primary. Jefferson wanted to reinforce the values of the revolution and build the most citizen-oriented government in the world.

THE FORMATION OF PARTIES

The Federalist Party would not be successful nationally after 1800, but the idea of a centralized approach to stability remains. Present-day liberals and Democrats have an agenda very similar to that of the Federalists' agenda. Conservatives and Republicans hold views similar to the goals of Jefferson. (Please note that although Thomas Jefferson is listed by the modern Democratic Party as one of its founders, this is true only in a strictly historical sense. The goals of the Democratic Party changed dramatically after the Great Depression.)

> **The Formation of Parties**
>
> Democratic-Republicans reflected the beliefs of early liberals, who valued freedoms, tolerance, and independent actions. Jefferson wanted to reinforce the values of the revolution and build the most liberated government in the world.

Washington tried to remain above partisan politics during his terms. The first great split was between Jefferson and Hamilton. Jefferson became the leader of the "liberal/radical" opposition, and Hamilton became the main spokesperson of the "conservative" Federalist government. Adams took on Federalist leadership during his presidency. Madison started as a great defender of the Constitution but ended as a supporter of Jefferson's approach, favoring weaker government.

The election of 1800 is considered the first major turning point of political power. The Federalists, under Adams's leadership, gave up power without a civil war to the hated Democratic-Republicans under Jefferson's leadership. Federalists would not win again.

❯ II. THE FEDERAL CONSTITUTION OF 1787 AND THE AMENDMENTS

Basics of Federalism

The nature of *federalism* has changed over the centuries. Prior to the Convention of 1787, many in the country used the term to describe a government where states had general control of rights and powers, with interstate problems being settled by a central authority.

Changes in federalism were extensive in the 20th century, especially after the Great Depression and World War II, leading to new demands for controls by the national government. Federalism has come to mean basic rights guaranteed by the Bill of Rights, leadership from the capital, and financial controls under federally funded mandates.

Federalism did come to stand for a stronger central government, yet early leaders such as Jefferson made sure that state controls remained intact. This was clearly reflected in judicial questions, where the Bill of Rights was defined as applying only to federal laws. State laws, and their inclusion of civil liberties, could differ from federal laws. The most glaring example of this was the right of states to claim to hold "citizens in bondage" (slavery).

The Constitution of 1787

The original Constitution contained eight basic parts: a preamble explaining the goals and seven articles defining the powers of the new government. The majority of the descriptions concern the legislature, which was considered the primary branch of government by the founders.

THE LEGISLATIVE BRANCH

Almost all details of specific powers are about Congress. Congressional officers, such as the Speaker of the House and President of the Senate, are specifically listed. Congress must keep a journal, control its own members, and hold powers over the executive and courts. Congress was given a list of 17 duties, covering items such as interstate commerce, regulating money, creating courts, declaring war, taking care of roads, awarding patents, counterfeiting, and making rules for the military. Congress also is limited by a "mini Bill of Rights" in Section 9. Congress cannot suspend certain rights without declaring emergencies, cannot tax exports, and cannot grant titles of nobility. Even though a president can step in and veto legislation, the entire legislation must be rejected, and Congress can vote to override the president's objections.

THE EXECUTIVE BRANCH

The president is commander of the military but must allow Congress to fund the military and manage its rules. The president appoints ambassadors and other officials and negotiates treaties, but both powers require congressional approval. The current use of the "recess appointment" power, where congressional approval is not immediately needed, is a rare event. Presidents can also be removed from office by Congress.

THE JUDICIARY BRANCH

Lower courts can be created to help the federal courts' workload, if Congress authorizes them. Federal judges and justices serve for life, unless they are impeached and removed. Federal courts have jurisdiction over cases involving state's suing or being sued. The rest of the article covers the issue of treason. Though this crime is defined very broadly in other nations, in the United States, treason can exist only if someone is "levying War against them [the United States], or in adhering to their Enemies, giving them Aid and Comfort."

Articles 4, 5, and 6 describe the relationship between states and the federal government, describe how amendments can be created, and establish the the supremacy of national law. Article 7 outlines the ratification process.

> ## The Constitution, in Simpler Terms
>
> The Constitution establishes the five basic forms of political authority that are central definitions of the government of the United States: leadership through representatives that serve at the will of the voters (republic), national and local levels of authority (federalism), different areas of authority for different leaders (separations of powers), forms of limits of power by having leaders control each other (checks and balances), and strict freedoms that cannot be removed from the public (civil liberties). The interpretations of the extent of these powers make up the basic political debates of our system.

Interpretations and Adjustments

The Preamble: The call for a "more perfect Union" showed that the existing government was a less-than-perfect union. The other goals of "justice," "domestic Tranquility," "defence" (defense), and "general Welfare" were clearly practical issues that were not being addressed during the turmoil of the early 1780s. The final call for "Blessings of Liberty" is a return to the goals of the Declaration of Independence.

Article 1: The original primacy of the Congress is demonstrated by the length and care given to this portion. Congress is given leaders, rules for organizing, and at least 17 duties. Furthermore, Congress is given the power to "make all Laws which shall be necessary and proper." This sentence has been given the title the "Elastic Clause" and has become one of the most important points of constitutional interpretation in the history of the United States. Clearly, the founders anticipated change and new challenges for this government. They did not intend to leave the national Congress with no powers to adapt to changing times. However, the scope of such adaptations is still debated.

Article 2: Much of this portion of the Constitution is given to the procedure by which the president and vice president are elected, which is known as the electoral college. Most of this section was amended by the 12th Amendment. What remains is a sketch of a presidential office of limited and checked powers.

Article 3: Article 3 states that there will be federal courts, that Congress can create them, and that judges' salaries are guaranteed, and it carefully defines treason. These are the basics covered in the article, and little else is present. The power of judicial review was given to the judiciary by the decision in the case of *Marbury v. Madison*.

Article 4: According to Article 4, states must give the various laws of other states "Full Faith and Credit," return fleeing criminals to other states, and give approval for new states to be carved out of their state properties. Some controversies have occurred when states strongly disagree about certain laws, such as the legality of gay marriage or the extradition of criminals to face the death penalty.

Article 5: Amending the Constitution can occur in four possible ways. Both the federal government and states must be involved. Congress can propose amendments with two-thirds of the votes in each house, or two-thirds of states can request that Congress call for a national convention for that purpose. Ratification occurs with the approval of three-fourths of state legislatures or three-fourths of the states approving through conventions called for that amendment. All amendments except the 21st have been created by Congress proposing and state legislatures approving.

Article 6: The "Supremacy Clause" is the label for this brief description of the "supreme Law of the Land" covering "this Constitution, and the Laws of the United States . . . and all Treaties . . . ." This clause also contains the promise to honor prior debts of the nation, which was important for the ratification debate. Leaders also are protected from having to make religious oaths as part of their duties to the government.

Article 7: Once 9 of the 13 states ratified the Constitution in 1788, the document was in effect. The new officers took their positions in the spring of 1789. Rhode Island, the one state that did not approve the Constitution in 1789, held a meeting to ratify the Constitution in 1791.

The Bill of Rights and Other Amendments

Anti-Federalists fought the approval of the Constitution, especially in New York, Virginia, and North Carolina. The major debate point centered on the lack of clear language showing the limits of power for this new federal system. The Federalists agreed to add a series of amendments as soon as the new Congress could form, and this was done in 1789. Madison, then a member of the first House of Representatives, led the development of the first set of amendments, which became the Bill of Rights

It is remarkable how little the Constitution has been changed since 1791, when the Bill of Rights was added. Only 17 other amendments have been adopted. Of these, 6 deal with substantial civil rights, and the other 11 are about procedures of government. The six rights are as follows:

1. Ending slavery
2. Due process and equal protection
3. Voting rights for all men
4. Voting rights for women
5. Voting without fees
6. Voting rights for those age 18 to 20

Congress has now included time limits to proposed amendments, especially because the 27th Amendment took 203 years to ratify. Since 1917, Congress has added a seven-year time limit to each proposed amendment, and this contributed to the failure of changes like the Equal Rights Amendment.

Basics of the Constitution

There were 55 leaders who worked on the Constitution, 39 who signed it, and 3 who stayed through the Convention but refused to sign. The structure of the Constitution is as follows:

1. Preamble: The goals of this new government
2. Articles: Seven major pieces, each describing the government and its duties
3. Sections: Organizing portions of the articles
4. Clauses: Paragraphs within the sections

Following are the five political principles of the Constitution:

1. Popular sovereignty
2. Federalism
3. Separations of powers
4. Checks and balances
5. Civil liberties via limited government

❯❯ III. FEDERALISM AND THE U.S. GOVERNMENT

Basic Structure of the Federal System

Federalism states that national and state governments share power and have both unique and overlapping duties.

THE ORIGINAL SCOPE OF FEDERALISM

The original view of U.S. federalism centered on the federal government and the state governments being considered relatively independent in their political powers. This structure of powers is known as dual federalism. The most obvious, most contentious issue in dual federalism was states' holding some "citizens in bondage" (slavery).

CHANGES IN U.S. FEDERALISM

One of the most fundamental and important changes in the government of the United States has been the gradual, but significant, redefinition of the federal system. As the federal government expanded its responsibilities, money distribution has become a central feature of its power. When the federal government helps distribute tax dollars to states, it attaches rules and regulations to those monies. States are left to decide whether they want to accept the needed funds and bend to federal rules or whether they would prefer to attempt to do without the cash and maintain their own legal priorities.

Under the U.S. federal system, power is shared between the national and state governments. The Constitution gives three types of powers to the national government: the delegated, the implied, and the inherent powers. *Delegated powers* are those powers expressly granted by the Constitution. *Implied powers* may be reasonably inferred from the Constitution by right of the "Elastic Clause." In the area of foreign affairs, the national government has *inherent powers* that don't rely on specific clauses of the Constitution. Those powers that are not delegated to the national government or denied to the states, are the *reserved powers* of the states. There are also *concurrent powers* that are held by both the national and state governments, such as the power to tax and the power to establish and maintain courts. Moreover, *prohibited powers* are denied to the national government, the state governments, or both. For example, the national government can't tax exports and states are prohibited from making treaties with foreign governments.

> ### The Supremacy Clause
>
> Article 6 of the Constitution states that the document, laws of the United States, and treaties under its authority shall be "the supreme Law of the Land." All officials of the country must give oaths to support the Constitution. States cannot use their powers to override the national powers.

FISCAL FEDERALISM

When the international economy collapsed in the 1930s, many reforms and expectations that started in the Progressive Era were expanded and made a central component of the duties of the U.S. government. The core of many programs was the distribution of monies to build dams, roads, and energy sources and to fund job programs, food supplies, and medical care. The federal government has become a source of support in many financial areas, and with this support, the federal powers are expanded. State and local governments must follow federal rules about discrimination, equality, and affirmative action.

Examples of National and State Powers in Modern Federalism

BASIC NATIONAL POWERS

The powers of the national government include the delegated powers to collect taxes, coin money, regulate commerce, raise and maintain armed forces, declare war, and grant copyrights and patents. An example of an implied power is the power to establish federal regulatory agencies, such as the Federal Aviation Administration. Among the major inherent powers are those to acquire territory, set immigration policy, and protect against domestic rebellion.

BASIC STATE POWERS

These reserved powers include the rights to conduct elections and select local officials and electors. Rights under the 10th Amendment and other traditional rights held by states include the following:

- Business licenses
- Marriage licenses
- Legal practice licenses
- Professional licenses
- Civil laws not involving federal issues
- Criminal laws not dealing with federal crimes

Major Interpretations and Events in Federalism

- 1789 to the Civil War—Dual federalism is dominant. The prevalent belief is that the federal government was given very limited powers by the Constitution, leaving the states with the most power. States can define full citizenship. Specific court cases are used to define federal authority over trade, interstate commerce, and banking.
- Civil War Amendments (1860s)—The 13th, 14th, and 15th Amendments take from the states the rights to allow slavery, define levels of citizenship, and stop African American men from voting.
- Post-Reconstruction (1876 to early 1900s)—States regain authority over the status of citizens in areas of voting and segregation, formalized in the 1896 case of *Plessy v. Ferguson.*
- New Deal and World War II (1930s and 1940s)—Federal authority over commerce is expanded during the New Deal and legislation after WWII. The Employment Act of 1946 is a key example.
- Civil Rights Era (1950s to the 1970s)—With *Brown v. Board of Education,* the Civil Rights Act of 1964, and the Great Society programs, federal authority over civil liberties and public welfare is expanded.
- Devolution Era (New Federalism) (1980s to the present)—Starting with the election of Ronald Reagan in 1980 and the Republican majorities in Congress in 1994, efforts have grown to limit federal controls and influence. More control is given to states. More emphasis is being placed on shrinking the size and responsibilities of the national government.

❯❯ IV. POLITICAL BELIEFS AND BEHAVIORS

Traditions of Citizen Behavior

The generally accepted goals of our political culture have revolved around some key assumptions: Citizens should be free to participate in government, and governmental interference should be as minimal as possible. The government exists to give help when needed. Citizens should be informed of the decision-making process, and leaders should answer to the public and provide laws and rules. Government offices should be used for public service rather than for self-aggrandizement.

A two-party system has always dominated the way the United States has pursued governmental goals, despite many changes in regional populations, economic developments, and party groups themselves.

The two major political viewpoints, liberal and conservative, stem from the same sources. The Declaration of Independence's goals, the Article of Confederation's failures, the Constitution's simplicity, and the layered powers of federalism contribute to the beliefs of those on both sides. Political leaders across the spectrum fundamentally agree to support the system of government, the goals of individual liberty, and the general hopes of the Preamble's outline of the reasons for the government. What leads to disagreements is the possible ways that the government and citizens can most efficiently reach those goals.

Viewpoint Origins

The support of the goals of limited government runs deep in American culture, so as a result, governmental powers were designed to be limited. The addition of the Bill of Rights addressed public cries for less government and politics, not more. In the earliest days of the republic, American liberals and conservatives resembled their European counterparts. Conservatives wanted a more centralized system, a bit more elitism, and a focus on stable trade. Liberals were influenced by the fervor of revolution, local controls of power, and independence. Those who wanted more centralized control opposed those who wanted states' rights, no national banks, and private enterprise.

By the mid-1800s, the Jeffersonian vision of states' rights had become mainstream, and early Republican calls for national control became almost radical. After the Civil War, support of federal authority became the mainstream, until both major parties found themselves shocked by a rising tide of calls for help for workers and farmers. The once-radical notions of national transportation systems, federally controlled banks, and progressive taxes were barely being debated.

The ideological splits of the 20th century were highlighted by responses to the Great Depression and civil rights movement. Liberals became the champions of national controls of economic policies, social welfare, and civil liberties. Conservatives took over the agenda of free enterprise, states' rights, and governmental controls of many moral issues. Yet there were many periods in U.S. history in which third-party leaders continued to attack both dominant groups as being nearly identical in leadership.

Participation and Voting

Possibly the most critiqued issues of U.S. political behaviors are voter participation and election turnout. While socio-economic characteristics influence voter participation, three factors most influence how voters make decisions: candidate appeal, party identification, and issues. A candidate's personal appeal has always informed voter behavior as is evidenced by the election of many military heroes to the presidency. Party identification, however, is the most accurate predictor of whom people will vote for. People tend to vote loyally for the candidates of the party they most closely identify with. For many voters, issues such as the economic conditions in the country determine which candidate they will vote for. However, the fact that modern voter turnout continues to drop is troubling. The greatest fear has been that citizens have grown so indifferent toward their leaders that they have stopped bothering to vote.

Declining levels of political participation and voter turnout are often attributed to disillusion with the political system because of perceived effectiveness of participation and voting in changing policy decisions. On the more positive front, reforms have started to make voter registration quicker and simpler. Family influences, educational levels, age, and economic conditions continue to influence who votes, even if these factors do not influence how they vote. With websites, viral campaign videos, and celebrity endorsements, younger voters are being educated through the Internet and inspired to register and to vote.

Participation and Civic Responsibility

Civic participation for the good of the community is a long-standing tradition and practice in the United States. Civic participation is very political in nature because community groups themselves are considered independent vehicles of change, bias, and party support.

Religious groups work in civic areas for public assistance, social events, and issue lobbying. Education and youth groups exist to give young people new opportunities and share in the learning of cultural and political traditions. Medical volunteer groups become advocates for many agency policies concerning public health. Business groups become powerful agents for political contacts, issue guidance, and public debates. Many groups exist just to give advocacy assistance to those with similar political goals. Environmental issue groups also play key roles influencing policy trends toward business actions. All of these groups are founded on similar principles that require individual citizens to try to make a difference in society. They are made possible by individuals making the choice to participate, the lack of large-scale governmental control of such groups, the ability of such groups to determine their own causes, and the ability to try to influence policy makers. One of the biggest changes in the way civic groups influence the national agenda has been how these groups lobby the leadership. More single-issue groups have emerged with the growth of the population and the expansion of legal forms of campaign influence.

The Political Spectrum

Socialism: This is the idea that the citizens of a republic can select large parts of the economy and issues of social welfare to be controlled and organized publicly by the government. Socialists believe that this should be done for the benefit of all citizens. The universal public education system in the United States is an example of a socialist system.

Liberalism: Since the Progressive Era, and certainly since the Great Depression, liberals support the government taking a central role in economic development and social welfare. Since the Cold War, liberals have wanted to keep the government out of citizens' issues such as privacy, church and state relations, and free speech.

Populism: Populism is a political philosophy that supports the rights and power of the people in their struggle against the privileged elite. Modern forms include those who are more liberal on economic programs but generally conservative on social issues.

Conservatism: Since the late 1800s, conservatives have supported the ideas of competition and free enterprise with minimal government interference. Conservatives are very supportive of capitalism. They usually believe that freedom of competitive markets will create improvements and innovations for all.

Libertarianism: Libertarians in the United States occupy a curious position between liberals and conservatives. Libertarians are very supportive of the Jeffersonian ideal republic, where government provides as many freedoms as possible for both the economy and personal lifestyle choices.

Other Modern Terms and Concepts of Political Beliefs

Neo-conservatives (neo-cons): Many are the product of World War II and the Cold War. These modern, more libertarian conservatives emphasize using U.S. economic and military power to bring democracy, free enterprise, and human rights to other nations.

Bible Belt conservatives (theo-cons): A product of the civil rights changes in the South, these conservatives tend to be Southern Baptists and more fundamentalist Christians. They dislike central government yet support issues such as prayer in public schools. Christian voters see liberalism as attacking family values and personal independence.

Dixiecrats: This is the label given to white Southerners who remained very conservative but were loyal to the Democratic Party from about 1880 to 1980. The emergence of the Republican Party in Southern states has become a major feature of the "political realignment" that has changed the respective dominance of the two parties.

New Deal liberals: These groups tend to favor a central role of the government in the economy. They support unions, support Social Security as a safety net system, and generally want the government to take a leading role in economic welfare.

Progressives (feminist liberals, environmentalist liberals, civil rights liberals, etc.): The civil rights struggles, the environmental movement, and reactions to Vietnam and Watergate created groups that wish to have the United States lead in the creation of social equality and environmental protections. They tend to distrust big business and the major party leaders.

Rust Belt: Refers to the Northeast, which contains many of the traditional heavy industry areas and, therefore, has more union involvement than other areas. In addition, many of the most populated urban centers contain larger minority populations, making this area more liberal.

Sun Belt: The South and West are the faster growing regions of the country; they contain more nonunion areas, have a history of supporting states' rights, and are more conservative.

Farm Belt: The less populated but vast area of the middle of the country also extends to the ranching country of the West. Traditions of independence make this area conservative.

West Coast: Rapid immigration, pressing concerns over the environment, and more liberal lifestyle traditions make the area along the Pacific more liberal.

Southern strategy: Made popular by the Nixon campaigns, Republican strategies aimed to build a powerful and loyal conservative base in the Old South, denying Democrats one of their traditional core support areas. This strategy, which championed states' rights, was aimed at winning over white Southerners, who as former Democrats were angered over the changes brought about by the civil rights movement.

Major Shifts in Political Labels in the United States

The terms *liberal* and *conservative* have long histories. *Liberal* has been associated with the "left" at least since the French Revolution. The same is true with *conservative* and "right." What has changed, often dramatically, is the goals of party groups and their association with these labels. When the Constitution was adopted, national concerns focused on rescuing the economy, strengthening federal powers, organizing better national controls, and building trade with a more conservative England. As a result, those who led the government tended to want conservative dominance, meaning a strong central government and less reliance on weak states. Hamilton's calls for fiscal controls of states were key. Liberals then became the outsiders, calling for more emphasis on individual liberties. By the mid-1800s, the liberals had become the political status quo, with conservatives mostly concentrated in the cities of the Northeast.

When the party systems were breaking down before the sectional chaos of the 1860s, liberals were again the ones calling for changes. The long dominance of states' rights and local laws was falling apart, and liberals now wanted to go to more central controls in the name of justice and order. During Reconstruction and the Gilded Age, business independence arose, leaving the dominant political conservatives re-emphasizing local and individual freedoms. Liberals now wanted direct government control of workers' rights, property rights, and voter rights. This Populism and Progressivism would be absorbed by both major parties around 1900, with Teddy Roosevelt standing as the major progressive/liberal voice from within the dominant Republican Party.

The early 20th century saw the development of U.S. international powers, both militarily and industrially. After 1912, conservatives rejected Progressivism as a mild version of communism, and liberals embraced it as a form of workers' rights. The modern division between liberal views of the government's role in the economy and conservative views of laissez-faire capitalism were solidified by the politics of FDR, the outbreak of World War II, and tensions between capitalism and communism.

Civil rights reforms caused shifts in U.S. liberalism as minority rights campaigns created the basis of activism on women's rights issues and then environmental concerns. Because many environmental problems were seen as industry and corporation problems, these liberals oppose lenient controls over the powerful business sector. Conservatives chafe at national dominion over cultural issues, business decisions, and economic assistance to some. The late 1900s saw the re-establishment of conservative dominance, when it appeared that the federal government had successfully put into place the legal structures to ensure civil rights and could stop expanding so many powers. The 1980s and 1990s were times of massive economic expansion that strengthened the calls for less interference in the economy and peoples' lives.

Political Efficacy and Changes in the United States

Political efficacy is the study of how citizens view their own political beliefs, how they understand the political system, and if they believe that the system can change their lives.

Family background—This remains the most influential reason for political beliefs. Voting patterns show that the level of political interest, voting habits, and biases toward liberal or conservative views are formed by family traditions and behaviors.

Religious affiliation—Growing numbers of voters use religious tenets as guides for their political interests. Traditional beliefs of religions, interests in political activities, and levels of concerns are key. Those religions that emphasize stricter doctrines often see liberal or conservative goals as personal or moral threats.

Gender—With the traditional dominance of men in the business community, the trend still holds that men are more conservative in economic politics. Women have created strong majorities for social liberalism, although this varies from region to region.

Education—Studies indicate that those with higher levels of schooling tend to be more liberal. This clearly makes a difference in voting turnout patterns too. More educated voters cast ballots in much higher percentages than less educated voters.

Ethnicity—The history of immigration is a history of calls for social reforms, worker rights, and civil equality. Minorities tend to support liberal programs.

Economic status—The rich vote, and the poor don't. It is an ancient tradition that those who benefit the most from the political structure will go to great lengths to keep that control.

Voter Biases

The strongest factor in determining voter biases is party identification and support for major party issues. How the party appears to parallel an individual's beliefs about taxes, jobs, moral codes, family issues, and political freedoms is paramount to party identification for the individual. This has been shown to be the main reason for voting behavior, with almost no consideration given to the actual person running. As long as the voter believes that the candidate will follow the same beliefs, support is likely. The exception to this occurs when candidates of the same party are running in elections; then personality factors are primary.

Factors in U.S. Voter Turnout

Voter turnout in the United States is relatively low (especially in nonpresidential elections). Some factors may include the vast and diverse nature of the U.S. population and the relatively centrist politics of our major parties. Factors that may impact voter turnout are these:

- Crisis/war—Levels of patriotism, reactions to national threats, and panicked calls for help will bring out votes.
- Age—Senior citizens vote more often and tend to believe in the political system.
- Religion—Evangelical Christians are registering more voters, helping with drives.
- Income—Poor residents have never voted in high numbers.
- Region—Rural vote turnouts tend to be high and conservative, yet they are less important at the national level because of low population in these areas. Southern states are key to politicians with national ambitions due to extreme pockets of conservatism and trends of higher population growth.
- Urban/suburbs—More votes are now found in suburbs than in city centers. Suburbs tend to be whiter and are, therefore, more balanced between conservative and liberal than the minority-dominated city centers.
- Apathy—When platforms are similar or races are one sided, turnouts are reduced.

❯ V. PUBLIC OPINION AND POLLING

Introduction

Political scientists have defined the concept of "public opinion" as the ways that citizens of a republic evaluate leaders, candidates, issues, or institutions that control the laws and the government. Public opinion is critical to the ability of the leadership to gain supporters and voters.

The general political viewpoints of voters have remained stable and relatively moderate over the past decades, because U.S. citizens are comfortable knowing that the government is stable and centrist. When compared with citizens of other republics, Americans have fewer issues of control; a large part of the public even claims little interest in government.

In the same way, campaigns and parties tend to focus on "pocketbook" issues, sensing that the public raises its level of concern only when money and jobs are involved. Presidential elections certainly turn on such truths. For the entire 20th century, about two-thirds of all elections could be predicted on the rise and fall of election-year economic conditions. When unemployment and inflation were improving in the year of the election, the incumbent party mostly won. When unemployment or inflation were worsening, the incumbent party and candidate were in trouble.

This was proven true most recently in the 2008 election, with Democratic candidate Barack Obama defeating incumbent Republican party candidate John McCain in a time when the United States was in an ever-worsening recession.

The Development of Opinions

Political loyalties are created by way of political socialization. Surveys consistently show that the biggest factor remains family influence; that is, families most significantly affect a person's values, concerns, level of party loyalty, or sense of trust in government. Media presentations, on the other hand, are usually significant for short periods of time and in extremely close elections.

Another important feature of political socialization is a person's level of education. Those who have advanced degrees are more likely to be involved than those with less advanced degrees. Job status is important as well; for those who may have lost economic standing due to a job change or loss, participation is high. Those who have always lived closer to the poverty level have very low levels of involvement and irregular voting habits.

Opinion Data

Modern communications have made the gathering of opinion data instantaneous. Political groups use this data to determine voting patterns, make economic projections, and gather money. Political leaders use it to test support levels, check issue priorities, and watch for potential conflicts, among other things. Television and the Internet, in addition to the continued use of the radio, have dramatically changed the nature of political analysis.

Many elements of government use opinion data. Presidential staff constantly monitor the popularity of the president, the influence of the president (bully pulpit), and the impact of presidential speeches. Members of Congress monitor the popularity of programs, potential legislation, and their image versus that of the president. Business markets monitor the confidence of the typical consumer and use that data for economic planning.

Presidents face consistent patterns in popularity. Right after a president is elected, the public always grants him or her a "honeymoon period." The president enjoys a great deal of popularity at that time and is expected to take the policy initiative. Congress is aware of the public's need for change and so often goes along. After about three months, the public begins to lose some patience and interest, and Congress becomes more independent.

The middle years of second terms are notorious times of low ratings for the executive. "Lame duck status" sets in, and support for presidential initiatives is low. Voters also begin blaming the president for problems that have not yet been resolved.

Polls and Polling

The business of monitoring the views of the public was developed after coast-to-coast forms of communication were invented. The process makes careful use of statistics and bias control. Polling, as it is now known, is a massive, lucrative, and controversial business used by all participants.

Both major political parties hire polling companies, each carefully trying to select results that will help its own party image. Party leaders manage which poll information is released to the media, when it is given, and how it is analyzed. In addition, poll data is used to convince supporters to increase levels of support and build party morale. Independent media analysts spend much time debating these political messages and their impact. Those who are aware of the biases worry about parties taking over control of data presentation. Others ignore data when it doesn't fit their ideas or those of the party they support.

Pollsters carefully monitor the public's moods and mastery of the parameters:

Distribution—How big a piece of the electorate is concerned about an issue? If a large or critical part of the entire electorate is strongly in favor of a particular issue, then consensus is reached, and that issue tends to be solved by all parts of government. If the electorate is evenly split, the issue will be addressed at a regional level or left alone. If the electorate is very fragmented or deeply divided, the nation is polarized. Polarized issues are often at the heart of party platforms in order to draw core supporters, but in reality, politicians and courts are reluctant to tackle them. That is because they only generate strong emotional reactions from the opposition.

Intensity—Gun control, gay marriage, public school prayer, and abortion are but a few issues that have uncompromising supporters and opponents. These issues are often called litmus test issues. Core party supporters use them to determine which members and potential candidates are trusted to be "pure" to the cause. Litmus test issues are frequently raised in the news when a Supreme Court appointee is being questioned by Senate leaders. True to form, the 2009 nomination of Sonia Sotomayor, a Latina judge, led to questions about race and reverse racism.

Latency—Leaders constantly search to understand what will move the public in the future, how they will react to possible changes, and how angry they will be if no change or resolution is attempted. Can the issue fade on its own, or will it develop into a crisis?

Salience—Some issues change in importance over time. Union rights caused massive conflicts and violence in the past, but they are no longer critical in most parts of the country.

Practice Section

1. The Constitutional Convention of 1787 involved all of the following factors **EXCEPT**

    (A) those who wanted a considerably more powerful government disagreed with those who wished to keep the Articles of Confederation.

    (B) representatives from states with big populations debated with leaders from states with small populations over the new structure of Congress.

    (C) leaders from Rhode Island refused to be present at the convention.

    (D) Anti-Federalists warned against the development of a new dictatorship.

    (E) Virginia's representatives primarily sought a parliamentary system.

2. The *Federalist Papers* were

    (A) written to convince citizens that the Constitution would appropriately limit the powers of the new federal system.

    (B) meant to persuade the public that Jefferson and Adams would uphold the Constitution once they returned from Europe.

    (C) not successful in quelling the fears of opponents, who demanded a Bill of Rights.

    (D) important in swaying state votes in Virginia and New York.

    (E) skeptical of how the new government could be organized.

3. The creation of political parties in the early republic

    (A) can be linked back to the leadership of Washington.

    (B) was developed separately by early American politicians.

    (C) was spurred on by the disagreement between Adams and Hamilton.

    (D) was entrenched in English traditions of liberal and conservative perspectives.

    (E) allowed the Federalists a significant period of control.

4. Madison's function in the beginning of political development in the United States included all of the following **EXCEPT**

    (A) drafting the majority of the Constitution.

    (B) heading debates supporting the new government.

    (C) remaining devoted to the Federalist program.

    (D) helping develop the objectives of Jeffersonian Democratic-Republicans.

    (E) crafting an epic essay on the authority of the central government.

5. *Federalism* initially implied that

    (A) the national government would defend minimal rights in states.

    (B) state governments would have comparatively equal sets of rights.

    (C) the national and state governments would guard similar rights.

    (D) different levels of government would have unique types of rights.

    (E) states would become part of the union only if they accepted the Constitution.

6. All of the following factors are proof of the initial control of Congress **EXCEPT**

    (A) presidential veto rights.

    (B) the length and specificity of Article 1.

    (C) limits on presidential appointments.

    (D) presidential "recess appointment" powers.

    (E) All are examples of congressional dominance.

7. Which power was **NOT** specified in the Constitution?

    (A) The vice president's involvement in two federal branches

    (B) Congress's ability to pronounce the penalty for treason

    (C) Congress's power to filibuster bills to their demise

    (D) Congress's right to suspend writs of habeas corpus

    (E) Congress's power to tax products sold from states

8. A major point of contention between presidents and Congress is based on

    (A) presidents assuming powers given to Congress in Article 1.

    (B) presidents operating outside of their legitimate constitutional rights.

    (C) Congress's reluctance to allow presidents act as genuine "commanders-in-chief."

    (D) Congress's allowing presidents control over rules of the military.

    (E) Congress's denial of state protection in times of crisis.

9. In the beginning years of the republic, federalism was expected to

    (A) allow for powerful local governments.

    (B) promise general equality of laws throughout the country.

    (C) guard the overall freedoms of the nation.

    (D) promote voting by all eligible voters.

    (E) reinforce the power of the federal government.

10. One important objective of recent Republican administrations has been to

    (A) return more control of federal funds to states.

    (B) return more control of civil rights to states.

    (C) return the administration of policies to the states.

    (D) return more tax authority to states.

    (E) All of the above

11. Significant changes in the scope of federalism were a result of

    (A) states' inability to defend civil rights.

    (B) the failure of capitalist economies to steer clear of major collapses.

    (C) clashes between republics and totalitarian nations.

    (D) shifts in attitudes about the universal rights of minorities.

    (E) All of the above

12. Following the Great Depression and the civil rights era, interstate commerce powers of Congress came to involve

    (A) the movement of goods and services across state lines.

    (B) the movement of goods, but not of laborers.

    (C) the overall movement of goods anywhere in the United States.

    (D) activities connected to economic trade across states.

    (E) criminal acts within states.

13. U.S. concepts of liberalism and conservatism are rooted in

    (A) the support of a limited government that creates an improved society.

    (B) the goal of meeting the needs of liberty and safety.

    (C) conventional roles of central and local authorities.

    (D) upholding of the constitutional structure.

    (E) All are true for liberalism and conservatism.

14. Voter turnout in the United States may be waning for all of the following reasons **EXCEPT**

    (A) the increasing power of a few dominant groups that control Washington.

    (B) a lack of faith in civic participation by minority groups.

    (C) the vast expansion of the number of political groups.

    (D) the declining belief that participation in the government will even make a difference.

    (E) the opening of admission to campaigns to more political movements.

15. The most significant shift in U.S. liberalism has been

    (A) a change from localism to nationalism.

    (B) a transition to the northeastern part of the United States.

    (C) the development of the Populist Party.

    (D) the dismissal of Teddy Roosevelt by the Republicans.

    (E) the increased focus on women's issues.

16. The biggest transformation in U.S. conservatism has been

    (A) the move of Dixiecrats to the Republican party.

    (B) the rejection of Progressivism in the 1920s.

    (C) the shift from supporting national leadership to local leadership.

    (D) the appearance of religious leadership.

    (E) the increasing power of rural and western states.

17. In polling, the use of a random sample could best be defined as

    (A) utilizing complex math models in computer programs to determine calls.

    (B) guaranteeing that any citizen has an equal chance of being called.

    (C) involving no predetermined criteria for calls.

    (D) choosing all of the potential political groups to call.

    (E) allowing only computers to select who is called.

18. Last-minute polls often have results that are significantly different from those of earlier polls. This is most likely a consequence of

    (A) the use of large numbers of questions.

    (B) the use of different types of questions.

    (C) an increase in sampling errors.

    (D) the lack of appropriate questions.

    (E) a deficiency in random controls.

19. The political viewpoints of the majority of the country have been stable about all of the following **EXCEPT**

    (A) support for the two major parties.

    (B) a relatively low interest in politics.

    (C) a general focus on personal liberties.

    (D) a reasonable level of concern about job security.

    (E) a general level of mistrust in government as a whole.

20. National polling organizations are inclined to be

    (A) skewed toward parties.

    (B) relatively accurate.

    (C) inaccurate about presidential results.

    (D) governmental agencies.

    (E) All of the above

Answers and Explanations

1. A

Almost instantly, leaders agreed that the Articles of Confederation were beyond revision. The Constitutional Convention of 1787 included disagreements between delegates from states with large populations and states with smaller populations over congressional representation; leaders from Rhode Island who refused to attend; Anti-Federalists who feared the creation of a new dictatorship; and Virginia's leaders, who originally wanted a parliamentary system. However, none of the representatives supported keeping the Articles of Confederation.

2. C

In almost all states, supporters accepted the concept of a federal Bill of Rights. Choice (A) is not appropriate because the papers elaborated on how the new government could work and not necessarily be limited. While Adams and Jefferson were both in Europe at the time, choice (B) is not accurate since the *Federalist Papers* were not attempting to persuade the public that Jefferson and Adams would maintain the Constitution once they returned. Choice (D) is wrong because the essays probably did not influence votes in Virginia and New York; Hamilton appeared to have carried New York, and Madison's demands for a new system helped in Virginia's convention. Choice (E) is incorrect because the *Federalist Papers* were not criticisms about how the government could be organized.

3. D

The development of political parties in the early republic was founded in English conventions of liberal and conservative perspectives. English traditions of Whigs and Tories influenced our leaders significantly. Washington did not trust party conflicts; Hamilton opposed Jefferson, not Adams; and the Federalists lasted only two administrations.

4. C

Madison's part in the early political development of the United States included drafting the bulk of the Constitutional plan, leading debates upholding the new plan, helping develop the goals of Jeffersonian Democratic-Republicans, and writing the great essay on the powers of the central government. Choice (C) is the best answer because during the Jefferson presidency, Madison left the Federalist Party; he did not stay loyal to the Federalist program.

5. D

Federalism initially meant that different layers of government could have unique forms of rights. For example, rights approved by the federal government can be very different than those granted by the states. The national government would protect "republican" governments in states, but not all rights. States could, and did, have vastly different sets of citizens' rights. Approval from only 9 of the original 13 states was required for ratification and execution of the Constitution.

6. E

Presidential veto powers, the length and detail of Article 1, checks on presidential appointments, and presidential "recess" appointments are all legitimate rights of Congress. If the president vetoes, Congress can still override. "Recess appointments" must be approved after a year.

7. C

Congress's right to filibuster bills to death is tradition. Choice (A) is incorrect because the vice president is also president of the Senate. Choice (B) is wrong since the Constitution obviously states Congress's power to declare the punishment for treason. Choice (D) is incorrect because, according to the Constitution, Congress can suspend writs of habeas corpus in emergencies. (Congress can also declare emergencies.) Choice (E) is incorrect because Congress is not allowed to tax exports from state ports.

8. A

An important factor in power disputes between presidents and Congress comes from presidents assuming powers that were granted to Congress in Article 1. President Lincoln started many power trends when he managed to suspend writs of habeas corpus in the emergency of 1861. He claimed that Congress could not act, thus allowing him to take on Article 1 authority. Sometimes presidents' use of listed powers is controversial in interpretation. Congress has never criticized the president's leadership role as civilian commander of the armed forces.

9. C

In the beginning of the republic, federalism was intended to guard the general liberties of the nation's citizens. The system of layered government was, and is, designed to meet this objective. Choice (A) is incorrect because local governments do not need to be strong or to be equal to the federal government. Choice (B) is incorrect because federalism in the early days of the republic was not meant to guarantee the general equality of laws in the country. Choices (D) and (E) are incorrect because voting levels and stronger national powers were not goals of early federalism.

10. C

One significant objective of recent Republican administrations and majorities has been to return the administration of policies to the states. New federalism hopes to allocate more control to states regarding the creation of policies, even if they use federal funding. Choice (A) is incorrect because the goal is not to cut federal control of federal funds. Choice (B) is incorrect because the goal is not to modify civil rights. Choice (D) is incorrect because the goal is not to change the authority of the federal government to tax its citizens.

11. E

Major shifts in the scope of federalism were brought about by all of the factors listed. Choice (A) relates to the changes brought about by the Civil War, choice (B) refers to the shifts that resulted from the Great Depression, choice (C) refers to the Cold War modifications,

and choice (D) refers to the changes that came about during the civil rights movement.

12. D

After the Great Depression and the civil rights movement, interstate commerce powers of Congress came to involve economic trade across states. Choice (A) and choice (B) are wrong because they represent earlier interpretations of interstate commerce powers. Choice (C) is incorrect because it is not a correct description of the interstate commerce authority of Congress. Choice (E) is incorrect because criminal acts inside states continue to be under state authority.

13. E

The concepts of liberalism and conservatism are based on beliefs in limited government creating a better society, combinations of the need for liberty and safety, conventional roles of central and local authorities, and the support for the constitutional framework. These forces in the U.S. system have supported constitutional limited government since the beginning.

14. B

Civic involvement in the United States is not declining due to lack of conviction in civic participation by minority groups. Minority groups participate like all other groups. All of the other possible answers are accurate.

15. A

The greatest transformation in U.S. liberalism has been a shift from localism to nationalism. The other choices are also true but not as important to change as the shift from localism to nationalism in political motivations.

16. C

The most significant shift in U.S. conservatism has been the transformation from emphasizing national leadership to supporting local leadership. Again, this is the greatest change from this list; the other events listed occurred but were not as central to the development of modern conservatism.

17. B

Randomness presupposes that the polling group is aware of all of the potential population, how many people there are, and where they are located. These conditions must all be achieved in order for the sample to be accurately random. In fact, this is the most difficult part of high-quality polling.

18. C

Polls closer to a deadline tend to have troubles such as rushed data or skewed responses. Issues surrounding questions or controls are usually not at stake, in spite of the last-minute factor.

19. A

Support for the two current majority parties has shifted significantly. The other issues have principally stayed consistent among the population.

20. B

Major polls use very stable methods that have proven to be correct far more often than not.

CHAPTER 2

Influences on Elections

❯❯ I. POLITICAL PARTIES

Political scientists consider political parties as essential to a republic. Even though the general public has historically been wary of party groups and holds negative views about how they work, elections without parties are impossible. Countries that have numerous weak parties consistently have trouble making decisions.

Functions of Parties

The fundamental goal of political parties is to win elections, control the political system, and therefore push the party's agenda. They also do the following:

Create candidates and "label" leaders—Parties recruit leaders to nominate, fund elections, and support their viewpoints.

Influence voters—Parties try to build coalitions of like-minded citizens.

Gather funds—Parties raise hundreds of millions of dollars for their campaigns. The leaders create policies based on information they receive from their supporters.

Support leaders—Visits, calls, mailings, and other forms of group awareness can guide the agenda.

Build for the future—Parties must maintain loyal support by building policies that attract large groups for extended periods of time. Otherwise, influence would be fleeting and removed easily by later parties.

Act as watchdogs—Parties that do not have control of legislative or executive bodies are the leading critics of the party in power. They raise concerns over the policies and programs of the ruling party.

Run the government—Because Congress and the state legislatures are organized according to party affiliations, political parties play a major role in running the government.

❯❯ II. DOMINANCE OF TWO PARTIES

The Democratic and Republican parties have controlled the main political landscape in the United States since the 1860s. Their core supporters focus on basic interpretations of the Constitution, goals of government, and issues of personal beliefs. Third parties have occasionally gained pockets of support but have not been able to replace either major party or create a large national following. In part, this is because the Democrats and Republicans have been able to build coalitions that address the issues brought forth by third parties.

Another major feature of two-party dominance is the structure of national elections. Most states have rules allowing the established parties an automatic place on the ballot. New parties must raise large numbers of petition signatures to gain access, and even then, access is not maintained for future elections. The electoral college system requires parties to win the plurality of a state vote to get any College votes, thus making that occurrence rare for third parties.

One of the true strengths of the major parties is their ability to adapt, absorb, and expand. When the Republican Party was created, for instance, it was seen as radical and progressive. Democratic support of states' rights and local freedoms had become the mainstream. But with industrialization, the Republican party shifted its focus to promoting the growth of industry and took control of national politics for most of the late 19th and early 20th centuries. Both parties seemed "conservative" when confronted with the Populist and Progressive agendas, yet the parties eventually absorbed many of the policies and proposed programs of these third parties into their platforms, thus helping to maintain their grip on political power.

After the administration of Theodore Roosevelt, Republicans focused on businesspeople, reaching out to a nation exploding with wealth and industry. Democrats turned to the farmers and workers, standing in opposition until the Great Depression ripped apart business leadership.

Significant Party Changes

Outside of the two dominant labels, party support is much debated in political science. Voter loyalty has suffered for several reasons:

- The demise of powerful party machines in cities
- Smaller families
- The rapid movement of populations
- Decreasing reliance on public services in cities

Parties still hold certain key powers (finding candidates, pushing issues, and gathering funds), yet voter independence grew significantly in the late 20th century. Fewer ballots than before were cast for each major party. Republicans lost support in many urban areas and in the rapidly growing West. Democrats lost the farmers and the South. Millions would occasionally vote for protest candidates such as Strom Thurmond, George Wallace, Ross Perot, and Ralph Nader.

Future party alignments will probably hinge on continuing immigration. Hispanic American voters continue to grow in number, especially in the key electoral states of California, Texas, Florida, and New York. Will immigrants' traditional alignment with Democratic support for civil rights be broken up by religious concerns over abortion rights? Will the eventual rise of Hispanic workers into higher-wage jobs create a more conservative business orientation?

Brief History of the Democratic Party

Democrats claim a heritage stemming from the Jeffersonian coalition of the early 1800s. This coalition overwhelmed Federalists and dominated the country for decades. When regional interest split the Democratic-Republican majority in 1820, Westerners emerged as Democrats under the active leadership of Andrew Jackson.

Individual freedoms, frontier independence/states' rights, and agricultural interests were the basis of early Democratic coalitions. Support was mostly in the South and West (frontier areas). This gave Democrats an advantage, because the population was growing in these regions. There was also mistrust of wealthy elites in the coastal business areas, where class distinctions seemed counter to the spirit of democracy.

When federal troops left the South in the late 1870s, Democratic policies returned to states' rights and rural issues. Segregation gave power to whites and their socially conservative views. Some "liberal" support in the Northeast (e.g., Grover Cleveland) did exist, especially in urban centers where political machines influenced numerous ethnic voting blocks. Democrats built on this Progressive/Southern agricultural combination to win the elections of 1912 and 1916. After the 1930s, New Deal coalitions and economic liberalism flourished. Growing support came from organized labor, Northern African Americans, Northeastern liberals, and Southern farmers (e.g., for FDR). The public programs of the New Deal solidified the economic changes, and their Democratic supporters flourished with large majorities.

1945–1970: CIVIL RIGHTS ERA

Civil rights liberalism, Great Society programs, and the women's movement were dominant forces for the party. Southern Democrats became frustrated and protested with separate candidates in several elections. Informally called "Dixiecrats," these voters would still vote Democratic in other elections for decades.

1970 FORWARD

The Democratic party of the 1970s and 80s was an alliance among organized labor, urban dwellers, ethnic minority groups, intellectuals, and increasingly disaffected Southern Democrats. The election of Bill Clinton in 1992 was viewed by many as marking the emergence of a new Democratic coalition of labor, women, minorities, moderates, "Reagan Democrats," and the South. However, in the 2000 presidential election, the party's presidential nominee, Al Gore, lost to Republican George W. Bush despite having won a plurality of the popular vote. The party's fortunes improved with the 2006 congressional elections, which gave the party control of both houses of Congress, and again with Barack Obama's victory in the 2008 presidential election.

Brief History of the Republican Party

In the 1850s, Republicans were centrist and liberal reformers who emerged from the collapse of the Whigs and moderate Democrats. Party dominance can be classified in three major eras: the Gilded Age, the Roaring '20s, and post-1980.

ERA ISSUES/BELIEFS/SUPPORT AREAS

1854–1876, Lincoln Era—National leadership, emancipation, unionism, and reconstruction dominated the agenda. Support in the industrial North and the West Coast was sufficient for many electoral victories because the South was still in political chaos.

1876–1900, Gilded Age—Growing interest in expanding business and industry and support of the gold standard and "safe" money were dominant points of interest. Support in the North and West was massive, especially with rapid business expansion and exploding amounts of wealth available to leaders of industry.

1901–1912, Teddy Roosevelt Era—Roosevelt's goals included breaking up trusts and monopolies, along with the adoption of many Progressive ideas. Wide support outside the South was won due to Roosevelt's personal appeal and the popularity of his Progressive goals.

1912–1932, Business Era—Pro-business forces reduced Theodore Roosevelt's influence after 1912. Industry and wealth development became core issues in the face of isolationist reaction to World War I and growing concerns with communism. Strengths lay in the heavily populated Northeast. Leadership under Warren G. Harding and Calvin Coolidge flourished.

1932–1945, Anti–New Deal—Dislike of FDR and his programs was the beginning of a more libertarian approach toward federal authority. Republicans distrusted the increasing federal powers, especially in reaction against communism.

1945–1980, Post-WWII—Patriotism and intense anticommunist programs helped raise support. Issues about states' rights surfaced, as did opposition to civil rights legislation. The Southern strategy was used to gain electoral votes in traditionally Democratic areas (for Barry Goldwater in 1964 and Richard Nixon in 1968/1972). The process was dramatically increased with the landslide elections of Reagan in 1980 and 1984.

1980–Present, Reagan Era—Economic libertarians joined with social conservatives. Core support areas became the South, farm regions, and mountain states.

Parties In Decline?

One of the original strongholds of the political party was the rapidly growing urban center. Political "machines" took advantage of immigrants to dole out jobs in exchange for voter loyalty. Often corrupt, these machines built large party coalitions for decades.

Today, the corruption has been reduced, voting privacy protects voters, and party bosses have been eliminated. Some people believe that the two major parties are now in decline. Party loyalty is no longer critical for economic advancement, and easy movement across the country has fragmented loyalties, families, and connections. An increasing number of voters are claiming independence from parties. Polls show at least one-third of all voters today claim no strong ties to either party. Other pieces of evidence include low levels of voter turnout and the constant declarations by voters that they distrust parties and their leaders. The sudden popularity of candidates such as John Anderson, Ross Perot, and Ralph Nader is seen as evidence of a weak party structure.

There is, however, other evidence that parties are still strong and flourishing. Thousands of people readily give money to campaigns. Participation in meetings, demonstrations, message campaigns, and other party activities remains strong. Voter turnout among those who are registered is stable. When distrust in government exploded after Vietnam and Watergate, the influence of both parties began to decline. When conservatives resurfaced in the 1980s and 1990s, more party involvement occurred. With the parties diverging more and more, party loyalty may be resurfacing.

❯❯ III. CAMPAIGNS AND ELECTIONS

Elections in the United States are now noted for being numerous and open to universal participation. They are also expensive, especially at the statewide and national levels. They have become a game of the wealthy, lobby groups, and major parties. Television and Internet media dominate reporting, campaigning, and debating. Campaigns aim at controlling media presentations, spinning information to the benefit of their own causes, and avoiding any negative images. Recent elections have returned to 19th-century patterns of personal attacks, innuendo, and rumor. This appears to be increasing as campaigning through independent groups that do not answer directly to party controls grows.

Individual voters are not to be forgotten. Besides voting, they play critical roles in grassroots fundraising, lobbying leaders, and campaigning. Even with strict controls over personal donations, both parties have gained huge amounts of money through efficient contacts with one voter at a time.

Election Patterns

As mentioned in previous chapters, the two major parties have completely dominated national politics in the United States. They also tend to take turns dominating the political agenda for periods of time. Often, presidential elections are seen as focal points when parties create or lose dominance. Chapter 1 summarized how liberalism and conservatism have seen periods of control; the same has occurred for the Democrats and Republicans, as reflected by "key" elections.

The modern starting point is usually defined as the election of 1896. Traditions of traveling and campaigning, national media coverage, coordinated campaign staffs, and carefully managed candidates began with the contest between William McKinley and William Jennings Bryan. In 1912, there was a great Republican reaction to Progressivism, 1920 saw the rise of business and international neutrality, and in 1932 there was a reaction to the Great Depression. In each election, Democrats and Republicans traded places as the dominant party.

Civil rights issues began to dominate the election cycles after World War II. The beginning of the split of conservative Southerners from the old New Deal coalition began with the candidacy of Strom Thurmond in 1948 and grew with the candidacy of George Wallace in 1968. Reagan's victory in 1980 was the complete reversal of the great liberal landslide in 1964. The election of Barack Obama in 2008 was a return to Democratic dominance after eight years of the Republican George W. Bush administration. The elections have signaled the creation of the various party coalitions that dominate the political spectrum today.

The Role of Money and Reform Attempts

The influence of money in U.S. elections remains controversial. In a nation of over 300 million people with voter turnouts of over 100 million, campaigning is expensive, and costs continue to rise dramatically. Television advertisements are a main component of these costs, but radio, print media, and online media also play key roles in a campaign. With a large percentage of voters claiming little loyalty to the parties, images are critical to attracting "swing" or independent votes each election.

Money as a way of influencing politics is connected to a voter problem and a leader problem. If voters weren't as easily influenced by superficial images and emotional responses, then ads wouldn't be as effective; if voters were more critical in their analysis of the messages being presented, then attack ads and suggestive messages wouldn't as easily sway elections. There is also a fear that campaign contributions lead to policy changes, that those laws help only rich contributors, and that officials help only those who contribute. Even if it is not outright bribery, monetary assistance is still seen by many as an unfair, biased influence on the way the government operates. Attempts to control the flow of campaign contributions have increased for decades.

Efforts to make these contributions more public led to the creation of political action committees (PACs). This plan simply increased the money involved, however, because now PACs can legally build vast sums without hiding the details. Individual contributions are severely limited, but corporations and other powerful groups can "bundle" large numbers of such monies into one larger contribution. Internet communications have also allowed parties to reach millions of smaller contributors quickly and get money to many local races that never had such a level of national attention. Most recently, the greatest end run has been developed, that of "independent" groups creating vast ad campaigns that viciously attack "beyond" the control of a party or candidate.

At every turn, issues of large versus small, rich versus poor, and influential versus ignored arise. When reforms and limits are debated, a counterattack is mounted: the issue of free speech. Is giving money in and of itself a bad thing? Does a restriction on being allowed to help a campaign restrict the right of political free speech? Recent Supreme Court rulings, such as the controversial ruling in *Citizens United v. Federal Election Commission* that held that corporate funding of independent political broadcasts in candidate elections cannot be limited under the First Amendment, have sided with the idea that giving money is a form of speech; therefore, all proposed legal restrictions concerning campaign funds must bear this ruling in mind.

Presidential Elections

Party meetings, caucuses, and conventions once dominated the ways candidates were chosen. "Smoke-filled rooms," where insiders planned to support candidates under their influence, were the norm. Now, primaries that allow for the public to select local and national finalists for office flourish. For example, large conventions no longer select the presidential nominees; the nominees are usually chosen months before the conventions, during the flurry of early state primaries that commit party delegates to the public's choices.

These changes have certainly opened the process to more participants, but they have also created problems of money and strategy. Many states hold primaries early in the year, forcing candidates to try to gather vast campaign funds well before the elections. Lesser-known, though possibly very qualified, candidates are often eliminated quickly because they do not have the funds to conduct national campaigns in key state primaries.

KEY DIFFERENCES IN THE TWO MAJOR PARTS OF THE PRESIDENTIAL CAMPAIGN

To win the nomination means to capture the support of party regulars and loyalists. This often requires a more conservative (Republican) or liberal (Democratic) approach to issues and advertising. Issues and party platform stances are more critical. Special attention must be given to party groups that can make or break a campaign. Republicans must build a strong Southern base with issues like school prayer and family values. Democrats must gain enthusiastic support from unions.

To win the general election, the candidate must appeal to the interests of the general public. This might require the candidate to adopt a more centrist appeal without angering party loyalists. More emphasis is placed on personality and leadership. A powerful television image must be created. Quick quotes for brief impressions in the media ("sound bites") are valued. Polished answers to media questions and debate points are important in close races.

The Electoral College

The electoral college was created to avoid the masses selecting "demigods" and to act as a filter against mob rule. It was one of the final decisions of the Constitutional Convention, and little guidance was given as to who should serve in the important role. The Constitution forbids elected officials from serving during election years. Today, state party groups usually select well-known and loyal workers. Each state receives the number of electoral votes equal in number to its U.S. senators and representatives, for a national total of 538. (There are 435 representatives and 100 senators; per the 23rd Amendment, there must be 3 for Washington, D.C.—the same number as the least populated state.)

To win the election, a candidate needs 270 electoral votes. The largest state, California, had 55 electoral votes in 2004 and 2008. The smallest states (like Wyoming, for example) have 3 electoral votes. California has more electoral votes than many of the lesser populated states combined. It is possible for a candidate to carry the national electoral majority with the votes of only 10 states.

The votes are reapportioned after each census (this will be done next for the 2012 election, based on the 2010 census). States that grow faster than other states take electors from slower growing states. Selection of new electors is now usually done by state parties at state conventions. The Constitution states, "no Senator or Representative, or Person holding an Office of Trust or Profit under the United States, shall be appointed an Elector."

THE PROCESS OF THE ELECTORAL COLLEGE

New York used to be the largest electoral state but now stands third behind California and Texas. The popular vote winner (plurality) in each state gets all of the electoral votes from that party of that state (except for possible vote splits in Maine and Nebraska). "Plurality" means finishing first, without needing a majority of the popular votes. Electors are expected to vote for the popular vote winner, are bound by tradition to do so, and in some cases are required to do so by state law. However, electors are not bound by the Constitution to follow the state popular vote results. The Constitution protects such votes and would probably override any state laws to the contrary. Many electors have ignored their state mandates in the past, but none have ever caused a candidate to lose.

Electors meet in December, usually at their state capitol, and write their choices on ballots. Each ballot is sealed and sent to Congress, where the president of the Senate (the vice president) will open and count the ballots in January. The media does ask electors how they voted in December, and they usually answer.

If the electoral college does not have a majority winner, the vote reverts to Congress. The Senate selects from the top two vice presidential candidates, and each senator gets one vote. The majority vote winner (51) can then be sworn in as vice president. This way, a fallback leader is set if needed. The House selects from the top three presidential candidates, and each state gets one vote. (Washington, D.C., does not get a vote.) The winner is the candidate who receives 26 state votes. If no candidate gets 26 votes, the House keeps revoting until someone wins.

This event has almost occurred in close elections, such as in 2000. State congressional delegations may have a majority opposite of the public vote. Would the congressional party leaders vote for the opposition party candidate? This might have happened in George W. Bush's home state of Texas, where one of the more conservative electorates would have been contrasted with a slightly Democratic delegation in the House.

OBJECTIONS TO THE ELECTORAL COLLEGE SYSTEM

Many people object to the electoral college system; it is not a system of direct, popular election, and many feel that this is needed for modern times. They reason that voters are now informed enough and elections are honest enough to allow the people to control the votes.

The main controversy surrounding the electoral college is that the popular vote winner can lose the electoral vote. (This occurred in the presidential elections of 1824, 1876, 1888, and 2000.) This is seen by many as a miscarriage of the public's control, which is a fundamental principle of our government.

Others argue that the electoral college does not divide votes among states equitably. Some small states have a number of electoral votes that their populations should dictate. Others complain that the more populous states have too much influence due to their high numbers of electoral votes.

Campaign Finance Reform

National campaigns have entered the hundreds-of-millions-of-dollars range. There have been numerous debates about the need for such amounts of money, the sources of such funds, and the propriety of such collections. What promises are made for contracts, jobs, votes, or influence when so much money is involved? Many of these issues came to the surface during the elections of the 1960s, when television advertising became the central feature of modern electioneering.

Modern Campaign Finance Reform Efforts

Hatch Act, 1939: Federal employees and companies doing business under federal contracts were forbidden from contributing to elections.

Elections of 1968 and 1972: Reaction to "slush funds," secret accounts, and money Watergate used for illegal acts gave rise to federal reforms of money collections.

Federal Election Campaign Act, 1971: Controls were set on spending of funds, and 1979 Election Commission (FEC) was created for oversight, disclosure rules were set, and monies for primaries were controlled.

Buckley v. Valeo, 1976: In this Supreme Court challenge, the Court allowed Congress to control some contributions to candidates but protected other forms of funding to parties, as forms of free speech.

McCain-Feingold-Cochran Reform Bill: Efforts were made by Congress to limit "soft money" contributions (Bipartisan Campaign Act, 2002) and the influence of PACs.

Key Terms of Campaign Finance

Political action committee: A group registered with the Federal Election Committee (FEC) that is organized to elect political candidates or to influence the outcome of a political issue or legislation. This attempt at reform in the 1970s actually funneled more money into campaigns (PACs) registered under the FEC. Is the money for label-specific candidates or just "parties"?

527s: IRS Section 527 allows nonprofits to remain unregulated by the FEC. This loophole allows organizations to collect money not "connected" with campaigns and use it for political causes.

Hard money: Money for specific candidates. The per-election limit is $1,000 per candidate for individuals and $5,000 for PACs.

Soft money: Money contributed to avoid reporting regulations for a campaign.

Candidate money: Funds from personal wealth. If a candidate accepts federal aid, such as matching funds, then the limit of "candidate spending" is $50,000 of the candidate's own personal wealth.

Bundling: Putting together "individual" funds into group checks. This is often done by companies using multiple employee contributions.

Basic Rights and Limits to Contributions

Individual contributors: Contributions to candidates for specific elections are limited in amount and must be reported. Contributions to party organizations are completely unlimited.

Political parties: There are restrictions on how monies can be spent for national campaigns, when ads can occur, and whether or not they can mention federal candidates. Parties can spend unlimited amounts on "party-building" activities.

Interest and lobby groups: There are now limits on spending monies on ads that mention candidates or parties but few limits on spending to promote "issues" that are key to the group.

Political action committees: PACs have limits on how much can be collected for campaigns of specific candidates and when the monies can be spent.

527 groups: They have discovered few limits on spending on ads that refer to the issues that candidates support or oppose or to the personal lives of candidates.

Candidates: There are limits on how much of a candidate's personal fortune can be used, especially if the campaign collects other matching federal funds.

Local and Congressional Elections

Local politicians and members of the House of Representatives come up for re-election frequently. Some local races may be annual events. House members stand for election every other year. This has created the "constant campaign." The positive side of this is that leaders must listen to their constituents, because corrections can be quickly made by the ballot. As a negative, campaign fundraising takes a large portion of the leaders' time and energy. Incumbents in the House usually have tremendous advantages by being able to keep in constant contact with important donors and committees.

Donors are reluctant to support challengers because a loss will cost them influence. Challengers have less time to plan and campaign inside the two-year cycle. With these pressures, House incumbents spend much more time making sure their constituents are being helped and "correctly" represented by their votes. They have fewer opportunities to be independent for any length of time. Senate races, especially in larger states, resemble presidential races in terms of the need for money and organizations. The Internet has also changed campaigns in both areas, enabling candidates to send more information to a national audience; this way, both parties can focus on key seats and key states. The practice of funding campaigns from out of state has increased dramatically in recent years.

❯❯ IV. INTEREST GROUPS, LOBBIES, AND POLITICAL ACTION COMMITTEES

Introduction

James Madison and other U.S. founders had negative views of groups trying to influence policy or votes of the leaders of government. Madison referred to "factions" in the *Federalist Papers* and hoped that the federal system would protect the government from excessive influence by such groups. He was particularly afraid that elites would gain control of states, blocking access to government by deserving minorities. Within the new constitutional system, protections from the central government would guarantee that no local force would shut out the freedoms provided by the republic. This key argument for the new system helped explain the need for layers of authority. It was also understood that citizens needed to be able to connect with those of similar goals, petition various leaders, and have a voice in decision making.

Current Views

Today, the public perception of interest groups continues to be relatively negative due to the great sums spent by groups to influence elections. However, interest groups run the spectrum of political beliefs and are essentially the most effective avenue for all citizens to make their voices heard by the government. Interest groups such as corporations often hire professional representatives to lobby for their interests in the national and state capitols.

The flourishing of so many interest groups has become an issue. Thousands of voices compete to be heard, but no one leader has time to hear them all. Conflicts revolve around which interest groups have enough money or connections to bend the ears of key leaders. How do they hold on to such power? Is the ability to donate vast sums of money the decisive factor among groups?

Functions of Interest Groups

Interest groups exist to sway the political leadership in order to have their issues heard or put into law. Interest groups use professional lobbyists to represent their causes. Interest groups allow citizens to network, fight for common goals, influence government, or help members. Some groups are religious in nature and want to extend the influence of religion in society and politics (the Christian Coalition). Other groups further the causes of minority citizens (the NAACP and the League of United Latin American Citizens [LULAC]). Famous organizations such as Common Cause argue for governmental accountability, and the Sierra Club furthers environmental issues.

The most powerful way interest groups try to communicate with the government is through professional influence peddlers known as lobbyists. Lobbyists prepare memos for Congress, meet and debate, give evidence at hearings, petition, raise campaign funds, and even draft potential legislation. Lobbies are notorious for hiring recently retired members of Congress and then using their inside experience to outmaneuver other groups. Suggestions of impropriety caused Congress to create rules requiring a waiting period before former members could begin such private consulting. Even stricter rules apply to former members of the executive branch who want to be hired to lobby their former agencies.

Because some major lobbies have vast resources, their influence over campaigns and parties remains controversial. Current examples include Republican connections to energy company lobbies and Democratic connections to union lobbies.

In addition to private organizations, local and state governments also engage in lobbying. Most states, cities, mayor associations, and governor coalitions are represented in the state and federal capitols. Foreign companies and nations also use powerful lobbyists and their money to try to influence trade pacts, military assistance, and foreign aid.

The proliferation of interest group activity also reflects a positive aspect of the American system of government. With over 4,600 political action committees registered, all kinds of groups and opinions have open access to public officials. Any group, mainstream or radical, has an opportunity to register, gather supporters and funds, and contact leaders.

Prominent Interest Groups (Also Registered as Lobbies)

To increase their membership numbers and have more connections to governmental agencies, almost all civic and interest organizations have registered as lobbies. Most also have created political action committees to donate properly to campaigns. These groups mobilize active voters, conduct letter-writing campaigns, canvass cities, and gather substantial campaign funds. Their lobbying arms have large professional staffs that influence legislation, draft legislation, and constantly work with members of Congress and the president.

American Association of Retired Persons (AARP): The very powerful lobby force of citizens over age 55 has tremendous clout on issues such as Social Security and prescription drugs. Seniors vote in vast numbers.

American Bar Association (ABA): This group represents the legal community.

American Civil Liberties Union (ACLU): This group of legal experts focuses on court issues that might change civil rights and civil liberties.

Amnesty International: This worldwide organization focuses on human rights issues and political rights abuses.

Chamber of Commerce: This group represents businesses all across the nation, and the lobby often represents builders, local industries, and local leaders.

Common Cause: This social justice support group lobbies for many liberal causes and an "open, accountable" government.

American-Israel Public Affairs: Support for Jewish communities, Israel, and minority rights are a focus of this committee.

American Federation of Labor-Congress of Industrial Organizations (AFL-CIO): This group heads the labor movement in the U.S. lobbying for worker rights.

Eagle Forum: This conservative group supports family values issues and laissez-faire economic policies.

Earth First!: This radical environmental group has been the source of controversial, violent protests, especially by splinter groups.

Heritage Foundation: This very conservative group started as a research center for policy and now lobbies Congress in favor of diminished bureaucracy and less government involvement in people's lives.

League of United Latin American Citizens: A group that defends the rights of Hispanic citizens, its influence is rising with the increase in the Hispanic population in the United States.

Mothers Against Drunk Driving (MADD): This rapidly growing organization quickly forced major changes in many state laws concerning the penalties for driving under the influence of alcohol.

National Association for the Advancement of Colored People (NAACP): For over 100 years, this organization has been a voice on behalf of African Americans in civil rights issues.

National Rifle Association (NRA): Focusing on Second Amendment rights, this rich and powerful lobby has conservative and anti–big government roots.

National Right to Life Committee: This issue-oriented group seeks to make abortion illegal.

National Organization for Women (NOW): Central in the failed attempt to pass the Equal Rights Amendment in the 1970s, NOW continues to support women's rights and generally takes liberal positions, such as supporting legal abortion.

People for the Ethical Treatment of Animals (PETA): PETA tends to be against big business because of its use of animal testing for many products.

Sierra Club: This long-standing environmental group focuses on conservation of wildlife, cleanliness of air and water, and the use of land in the United States.

Lobby Group Basics

Almost all of the major interest groups have offices in Washington, D.C. They employ professional lobbyists who work with Congress. The lobbyists' goal is to create legislation that helps the interests of the members of the group in question.

LOBBYIST ACTIVITIES

Testify—Lobbyists attend congressional committee hearings and bring their biases and points of expertise. They have things to say about the possible impact of bills, especially for or against the goals of their group.

Meet—Personal contacts are critical ways to make political arguments. Controversial versions of such meetings are paid junkets, where lobby organizations pay for trips and vacations for members of government. Open bias and bribery sometimes occur.

Research—Lobbyists and their staffs have time and resources to gather data and issue reports that can sway members of Congress when bills that the lobby supports or opposes come to a vote.

Lead—Lobbyists can sway the masses within the organization to call and write to members of government.

Fund—Possibly the most powerful action is the raising of campaign funds.

Litigate—Lobby leaders can turn to the courts to attack acts, rules, and regulations that they feel are unfair to their group.

Political Action Committees (PACS)

When interest groups want to support specific candidates or parties, they may do so through PACs. The committees register with the Federal Election Commission and then may give financial support to candidates. PACs may give money directly to candidates' campaigns. This is called hard money and is closely regulated by the Federal Election Commission. Even with these rules, millions of dollars are given in this manner.

PACs also give money to parties. This is called soft money. Limits to soft money donations and expenditures are a subject of constant debate. Committees can use their money to create ads or messages for "issues," without specifically supporting a particular candidate. These kinds of expenditures are unregulated, even when it is clear that a particular candidate is being supported.

❯❯ V. MEDIA AND ITS FUNCTIONS

The History of Media

The media's effort to present political information is as old as U.S. politics. However, the idea that the media should be neutral and unbiased is as much a 20th-century concept as radio and television. Essays, leaflets, and books dominated colonial times and were often printed to sway the opinion of the general populace. The advent of daily papers aided in the distribution of news, but early newspapers would be considered quite biased by today's standards. Radio and television allowed for instantaneous news broadcasts, allowing a person on the West Coast to see or hear a political speech on the East Coast as it happened. But the Internet truly transformed the way in which people received their news. Instead of choosing from two different newspapers, or from among the major news networks, people could select from a seemingly infinite pool of news websites, government reports, political journals, and personal blogs.

Today, the media is as much a part of American political life as the three branches of government, earning it the nickname "the fourth branch." This is not to be confused with the large government bureaucracy, also called a "fourth branch" by some texts and references. Political parties, through selective use of the media, present their biases, advance their propaganda, and attack media groups they see as biased against them. Media leaders must juggle the needs for profit, competition with other sources, and the difficult task of staying impartial. Added to the mix are governmental regulations requiring certain kinds of "equal time" for political ads.

During the first presidential campaigns, political writers worked for party leaders, and the goal was to present an agenda and attack opponents, often viciously. What the supporters of John Adams and Thomas Jefferson said about each other was certainly not balanced or neutral; in fact, it was often openly slanderous.

These trends continued late into the 19th century, when the telegraph and transcontinental transportation allowed early media companies to expand nationally. Essays and pamphlets were replaced by newspapers and magazines. Newspapers such as the *New York World* and the *New York Journal* used scandalous headlines and salacious stories to attract readers. With growing newspaper circulation came growing influence. Publishers like William Randolph Hearst and Joseph Pulitzer used their newspapers as a platform to propagate their biases and to prevent the spread of opposing viewpoints. When illustrator Frederic Remington requested to return home from an apparently uneventful stay in Cuba during the Spanish-American war, Hearst famously responded, "You furnish the pictures, and I'll furnish the war." Throughout the late 19th and early 20th centuries, newspapers and their editorial staffs overwhelmingly favored Republican candidates.

The invention of radio and television created a vastly different perspective on news and the media that presented it. With their faces and voices on a national stage, journalists could become national stars themselves. Men and women such as Walter Cronkite, Edward R. Murrow, and Barbara Walters became household names, translating stardom into profit and influence.

Since the 1960s, the media has been increasingly viewed as having a liberal bias as a result of its coverage of the Vietnam War and the Watergate scandal. However, the early years of the 21st century have seen the perception of media bias shift to the right with the rise of such organizations as Fox News.

Goals and Concerns of Modern Media

What is the continuing power of the media? Why are biases so controversial? Can journalists balance the needs of profit, corporate demands, and personal integrity? The primary medium through which news is broadcast has changed from the newspaper to the television. Newspaper articles, which can number several thousand words, rely on thorough reporting, descriptive language, and an abundance of quotes from primary sources to create a relevant story. Televised news does not need to delve as deeply into an issue. The old adage goes, "A picture is worth a thousand words." And in the case of televised news, it is correct. Famous images, such as Neil Armstrong's first steps on the moon or the lone Tiananmen Square protestor defying a column of tanks, don't need much of an explanation; the footage provides its own.

The change in format from news articles to news broadcasts drastically shortened the amount of time necessary to present a news story. People were no longer relegated to reading about an event after it happened. They could now see and hear an event live, often as it was happening. Unfortunately, as the daily news became more entertaining, many important stories on government policy, which did not benefit as greatly from live television, began to be considered boring and sometimes difficult to watch.

The Internet is the new frontier of media presentations. Traditional media, such as magazines, newspapers, radio, and television stations, have the advantage of huge archives, time-tested credibility, and adequate funding to take advantage of the Internet. However, lone bloggers and small upstart groups can also take advantage of the Internet's inherent accessibility.

Influence of the Internet

As people demand more content in less time, the popularity of Internet-based news organizations has grown. Finding news on the Internet can be summed up in the phrase "what you want, when you want it." Vast numbers of articles, public records, and video segments are available for immediate consumption. Another benefit of the Internet is the global reach of its content. While a newspaper can be printed only a finite number of times and distributed to a limited number of locations, an online version of that same newspaper can be viewed by people anywhere there's an Internet connection. Unfortunately, the power to disseminate information can also be harnessed to disseminate disinformation. Rumors can be generated in seconds, hoaxes abound, and opinion is often confused with news. The issue of accuracy among many of the more independent news sources is a growing concern. This is especially true of blogs. Established news organizations have editors and large staffs that can verify reports and confirm accusations. What level of truthfulness is available on the thousands of individual Internet outlets?

Manipulated Media

The media has also become a tool of the president and Congress. Playing to the camera has become almost as important as a candidate's actual platform. Speeches are carefully orchestrated to meet C-SPAN coverage times, whether or not anyone else is in the chamber. Press conferences are completely controlled by using teleprompters, limiting questions, and allowing only selected persons to ask questions. Both the House and Senate have media rooms to which leaders and reporters can race for immediate coverage.

Media Bias?

Conservative groups have long held that the American media is very biased toward liberal issues and candidates. This stems from coverage of Watergate and the Vietnam protests. The main targets of such criticisms have been television reporting and lobbying done by actors who are given significant attention by the media. Polls taken by conservative groups claim that the vast majority of reporters for television and newspapers regularly vote Democratic. Polls taken by moderate or nonpartisan groups show that the media is relatively neutral and personal voting habits do not significantly influence coverage.

Clearly some media outlets tend toward different ends of the political spectrum, but the bulk of reporting attempts general neutrality. Though the mainstream media generally tries to avoid biased coverage, there are distinct pockets of support for conservatives and liberals, such as talk-radio programs, and public access programs. Periodicals such as the *Nation*, *National Review*, the *Weekly Standard*, and the *New Republic* exist to support certain biases. Nationally syndicated columnists such as George Will and Jim Hightower are famous for thoughtful defenses of political sides and issues. Uncensored programs on satellite radio help to perpetuate biases.

Effects of Media Roles in Modern Politics

Politicians and their staffs attempt to control the images presented in the media.

- White House staff members shield the president from many questions and control when questions are asked, how they are asked, and who asks them. Presidents universally use hidden prompts, earphones, charts, and other aids. so they appear more prepared and in command.

- Campaign appearances are now completely crafted down to the finest detail. The public sees only what has been thoroughly planned by the campaign staff—nothing else.
- Staff groups who try to control every image and trend also orchestrate election debates. Only certain questions are allowed, and each campaign team spends days in practice.
- Special media rooms, created by congressional leaders, afford them instantaneous access to news programs.
- Debates and speeches are timed to take advantage of news hours or C-SPAN coverage times. C-SPAN has at least two channels on most cable and satellite outlets that do constant reporting of the activities of Congress.
- Press conferences are usually held only when issues can be introduced in a positive manner.
- Presidential staffs have created a constant campaign that presents the president in favorable places and at key events in order to keep popularity polls at their highest. It is as if the election campaign never stops.

EFFECTS OF MEDIA AND TECHNOLOGY ON CAMPAIGNS

The national reach of news reports, combined with universal access to the Internet, has had a major effect on elections and leadership roles.

- Candidates use websites for national attention and fundraising. Elections that used to be relatively local in scope can now target a much wider audience and collect money from across the nation.
- Attacks on political parties and candidates have escalated dramatically through the use of the Internet, particularly through blog sites. Any and every group can disseminate propaganda to a vast audience, without much control of facts or biases. Rapid access to data and rumors gives many such groups the advantage of speed over traditional news groups.

MEDIA AND THE SHRINKING ATTENTION SPAN

The dominance of television and video images has dramatically reduced the amount of time spent presenting issues and candidates. Instead of presenting an entire speech, news organizations will use only the most relevant snippets of sentences, a technique known as "sound-bite news." Since the 1960s, the time spent by the media reporting candidate's speeches has dropped from units of about a minute to bites under 10 seconds. Media presentations are about key words, quick impressions, and flashes of faces. As a result, campaign staffs focus their efforts on allowing only quick messages, memorable lines, or quotes. Much effort is also given to trying to find memorable mistakes by the other side, thus presenting a quick, but lasting, image of the other party. Being able to sum up an agenda in 10 words or less is key to pushing that agenda on the American people.

THE MEDIA AND THE "SETTING OF THE AGENDA"

Media outlets look for events and issues that sell well or offer controversy. These items often become the "crisis of the day" that politicians must address, or at least appear to address. The selection of such events can show a bias toward parties and leaders, change the directions of policies, or enflame public anger. Recent examples include "millions of missing children," "the ozone hole," "the debt crisis," and others. These are put on the front of agendas for a time and then seem to disappear if the media decides the story is no longer key or profitable.

Practice Section

❯ FREE-RESPONSE QUESTIONS

1. (A) Identify two key roles that political parties play in the politics of the United States.

    (B) Explain how the two roles you identified influence or control the political agenda of the nation.

2. The Democratic and Republican parties are broad coalitions of major voting groups.

    (A) Identify three of the major subgroups of each party's coalition.

    (B) Explain how beliefs of each of the party coalitions have a form of unity.

    (C) Explain why members of each coalition have major points of difference in goals.

3. Most efforts at restricting campaign contributions have generally failed.

    (A) Identify the difference between "hard money" and "soft money" contributions.

    (B) Identify two reasons efforts at restricting contributions have failed.

    (C) Explain at least one reason some insist that campaign-funding restrictions should fail.

4. Some say the electoral college is clumsy and misunderstood, and it is an anachronism.

    (A) Explain two reasons the electoral college is still in place.

    (B) Explain two reasons the electoral college is opposed.

5. Interest and lobby groups have increased dramatically in number and influence.

    (A) Explain two reasons for the increase in interest groups and lobby organizations.

    (B) Explain two reasons why lobby groups have a bad image in historic and current public views.

6. Lobby leaders and lobby professionals wield many forms of power in Washington, D.C.

    (A) Identify three ways lobby leaders wield power with Congress.

    (B) Explain why these forms of power are effective.

7. The media has been described as a powerful force in influencing development of the political agenda of the government.

    (A) Identify three ways in which the president or Congress attempts to control media access.

    (B) Explain two ways the media appears to achieve so much influence.

8. The impact of media coverage has varied and changed over the history of U.S. politics.

    (A) Describe any two of the periods of media coverage.

    (B) Describe a goal of the media in trying to affect/bias the political agenda.

Answers And Explanations

1. **4-point Rubric**

   2 points in part (A): (identify two key roles)

   - Find candidates.
   - Influence the public.
   - Gather money.
   - Support those in office.
   - Provide for opposition to the majority.
   - Build political agendas.

   2 points in part (B): (explain)

   - Parties look for qualified candidates who can get elected, and then they support and train the candidates.
   - Parties get the message of the party platform out to the public, provide information, run ads, etc.
   - Parties raise funds that can be used for ads, flyers, etc.
   - Parties can be message leaders, and they can support other party members across the country.
   - Parties can band together as the "loyal" opposition to force compromises.
   - Parties canvass members for future issues and seek solutions to problems.

2. **10-point Rubric**

   6 points in part (A): (three groups in each party identified)

   - Democrats: African Americans, union members, liberal progressives, the "New Left," feminists, Hispanics.
   - Republicans: Neo-conservatives, upper class, supply-side conservatives, Christian Coalition, Southern conservatives, Westerners.

   2 points in part (B): (points of unity)

   - Democrats: Economic guidance by government, civil rights for minorities, pro–environmental programs, pro–worker rights.
   - Republicans: Economic privacy, states' rights, pro-business, less government.

   2 points in part (C): (points of difference)

   - Democrats: Hispanics may be less loyal due to religious beliefs, splits over civil rights agendas, splits between unions and feminists.
   - Republicans: Splits over religion, emphasis on business and taxes, North versus South.

3. **4-point Rubric**

   1 point in part (A): (hard contributions versus soft contributions)

   - Hard money contributions are regulated contributions given directly to candidates for their campaigns; soft money contributions are less-regulated monies given to parties for activities such as "party building."

   2 points in part (B): (two reasons restrictions have failed)

   - There are too many loopholes.
   - Party building can be pro or con toward a candidate.
   - There are no limits on contributions not controlled by parties.
   - There is little incentive to change for those in office and benefiting from current rules.

   1 point in part (C): (one reason restrictions should fail)

   - People should be able to spend their money.
   - Restrictions penalize the wealthy.
   - Free speech would be limited.

4. **4-point Rubric**

   2 points in part (A): (two reasons the system remains)

   - Large states benefit.
   - Reduces costs of campaigning everywhere.
   - Cuts potential of vote fraud in every precinct.
   - Creates greater majority than popular votes.
   - No replacement system is a real improvement.

   2 points in part (B): (two reasons to oppose)

   - Is too biased toward large states.
   - Is too biased toward states dominated by one party.
   - Is biased against small parties.
   - Blocks the public's votes.

5. **4-point Rubric**

   2 points in part (A): (why an increase in lobby groups)

   - Is now legal to give campaign money.
   - Is also legal and encouraged to register and to lobby.
   - More issues and single-issue groups exist.
   - More groups exist outside of two political parties.
   - There is a more diverse population to represent.

   2 points in part (B): (why a negative image)

   - Are too locally dominant.
   - Suppress minorities.
   - Are too divisive.
   - Are too controlling of a few leaders.
   - Are too powerful if wealthy.
   - Are too likely to bribe leaders.
   - Are too controlled by wealth and contributions.

6. **6-point Rubric**

   3 points in part (A): (three forms of influence)

   - Testify.
   - Contact.
   - Research.
   - Lead the group.
   - Fund campaigns.
   - Go to court.

   3 points in part (B): (explain why powerful)

   - Have access to committees in Washington at critical debate times.
   - Exercise great control and influence one-on-one.
   - Have expertise and staff resources that even Congress might not have.
   - Are representative of large groups with many followers and lots of money.
   - Exercise tremendous influence over who gets elected or how easy it might be.
   - Have the funds and data to go to court and sue (deep pockets).

7. **5-point Rubric**

   3 points in part (A): (ways leaders attempt to control the media)

   - Carefully managed press conferences.
   - New leaks to select members of the media at key times.
   - Timed interviews, reports, access via government-run studios.
   - Campaign strategies and sound bites.
   - Carefully controlled debates.
   - Control of questions to be answered.
   - Control of who gets to ask the questions.
   - Party- and partisan-controlled Internet sites (blogs).

2 points in part (B): (how media gets influence)

- Selecting the stories to cover
- Selecting the bias of the coverage
- Controlling time given to stories
- Setting the agenda through control of issues/biases
- Controlling reports on the public's reactions/support

8. **3-point Rubric**

2 points in part (A): (periods of media coverage)

- Political pamphlets/essays that were for or against candidates
- Regional biases (slavery crisis)
- National corporate news to sell issues
- Radio/television news "from" leaders or for issues
- Internet reports from very biased and personal viewpoints

1 point in part (B): (goal of media in bias)

- Support specific candidates or parties because the media outlet agrees with them.
- Make money by selling crisis stories.
- Support political agendas, such as progressivism.
- Gain fame and wealth by exposing scandals.
- Earn money by finding an audience.

CHAPTER 3

Branches of Government

❯❯ I. THE LEGISLATIVE BRANCH

The House and the Senate

Congress was designed to be the branch of government that is most responsible for the development and maintenance of the republic, and for over a hundred years it was the only federal branch where to which the people directly elected members of at least one of the chambers (the House). Presidents were chosen by an aristocratic and elite set of electors; senators, until ratification of the Seventeenth Amendment in 1913, were chosen by state legislators; and justices were selected by the president and the Senate. Congress was also given the bulk of the duties listed in the Constitution.

DUTIES AND THE COMMITTEES

Congress exists largely to create laws. This critical duty is designed to be complex and deliberate, with the vast majority of potential ideas being rejected. Large-scale compromise is required, and the overall process is usually messy and lengthy. The job is also overwhelming. Congress attempts to deal with thousands of pieces of legislation each session, and no single member can master, or even read, all the details. Therefore, the committee system was devised to divide the duties into smaller units. Leaders of the chambers and committees must have strong powers to act as filters of legislative priorities and bring the bills to more controllable numbers.

Key Differences between House and Senate Powers

House of Representatives
- Initiates revenue bills (both chambers must still vote on the final version).
- Initiates impeachments of federal officials.
- Possibly requests discharge petitions for bills stuck in committee.
- House Rules Committee controls debate limits.
- Must have a speaker as leader.
- Selects the president if the electoral college can't.

Senate
- Holds trial for those impeached by the House and votes on removal.
- Can filibuster bills being debated.
- Riders to unrelated bills allowed.
- Informal leaders are party heads, with president of the Senate (VP) in a mostly ceremonial role.
- Selects the vice president if the electoral college can't.
- Approves the president's appointments to major federal posts and to the Supreme Court.
- Approves treaties initiated by the executive branch.
- Approves ambassadors as they are nominated by the executive branch.

The power to set the agenda and prioritize problems becomes immense. Congress is also expected to oversee other departments of government, represent the views and needs of constituents, help with military and foreign policy, and negotiate with the president and with some foreign leaders. It stands as an agency of oversight for national conflicts and problems, and congresspeople are ultimately accountable to their constituents, who elected them

Article 1, Section 8 lists the key powers of the federal legislature. Major powers include taxation, interstate commerce, declarations of war, and organizing the military. Interstate commerce regulation has become a major area where Congress has expanded its powers, because many tangential issues such as civil rights are connected to the business of interstate trade. Visit **http://www.house.gov/house/Constitution/Constitution.html** to review specific congressional powers in the Constitution. (Note that ASC = Article, Section, Clause.)

TRADITIONS AND PROCEDURES

Several traditions have been created under the order to determine the rules of congressional proceedings. The most significant are the traditions of seniority and majority rule in committees. In addition, the majority party chooses all committee chairperson positions, thereby guaranteeing that one party can dominate and shorten debates.

Within the Congress, differences between the House and Senate are noteworthy. Representatives must stand for re-election every other year, causing a focus on campaigning and money collecting. Because there are more than four times as many representatives as there are senators, the amount of individual power is reduced in the House. Senators also have much larger constituencies, and those from smaller states have greater influence than their counterparts in the House because in the Senate, every state has only two votes.

CONGRESSIONAL STAFFS, SPECIALIZATION, AND CONFLICTING ROLES

Because of all their complex duties, members of Congress must rely on dedicated staffs to shoulder much of the research, strategy formulation, and other tasks.

This has often isolated members from contact with voters and limited their abilities to become policy experts. Members don't have time to be experts on everything, are limited in the number of committees on which they can serve, and rely heavily on their staffs for briefings.

THE BUDGET

No duty is arguably more important than the development of the annual federal budget. The federal budget starts October 1 and lasts until the end of the following September, a period known as the fiscal year.

The executive Office of Management and Budget creates the budget outline, but Congress must prioritize the thousands of items and vote it through. Congress is also in charge of creating the tax system that will fund the budget.

CURRENT STATUS

Even though its original mission was to dominate the federal system, the Congress of modern times has been superseded in the mind of most citizens by the powers of the president. Congress's slow pace often frustrates the public, and in recent times, Congress is often led by a majority of the party opposite to that of the president or has different parties in control of the two houses. All of these items have weakened the influence of Congress and lessened public support.

The Basics of Congress

The types of committees of Congress are standing, joint, select/special, and conference. Thousands of ideas for potential laws are generated annually. Citizens, lobby groups, state and federal agencies, executive leaders, members of Congress, and staff members all contribute ideas for potential laws. The only way for all of this to be organized is through a filtering system known as the committee system. Congress is responsible for the duties listed in the Constitution, especially the 17 clauses listed in Article 1, Section 8, plus all items "necessary and proper."

LEADERSHIP AND ORGANIZATION OF CONGRESS

The House of Representatives has 435 members, elected for two-year terms from state congressional districts, with seats being distributed according to state populations.

- The Speaker of the House (required by the Constitution) is elected by majority vote of members and, in modern times, has always been a member of the majority party. The Speaker rules on questions of parliamentary procedure, influences committee assignments, assigns bills to committees, appoints the part's other leaders, and presides over House debates.
- The majority leader is chosen by the majority party to plan its goals and set its policies.
- The majority whip is the assistant to the majority leader, representing the regular membership and functioning as agenda setter, group communicator, and issue planner.
- Committee chairpersons are from the majority party. Chairpersons help form the legislative calendar, committee hearings, and many bill priorities.
- The House Rules Committee can make or break a piece of legislation when it either restricts or loosens the time limits and scope of debates.
- The minority leader is the leader of the opposition, minority party.
- The minority whip is the assistant to the minority leader and liaison to the minority party members.
- The House Republican Conference guides GOP bills and agendas.
- The House Democratic Caucus guides Democratic bills and agendas.

The Senate has 100 members elected for six-year terms from the entire state (rather than from a specific district, as in the House); there are two senators per state, 33 or 34 elected every two years (staggered-term system).

- The president of the Senate (required by the Constitution) is the vice president and can monitor debates, count electoral votes, and vote to break a tie vote of the senators.
- The president pro tempore (pro tem) (required by the Constitution) serves when the vice president is not available. Generally, it is a ceremonial role given to the majority party senator with the longest tenure (seniority).
- A majority leader is elected by the majority party to lead procedures and make committee assignments.
- A majority assistant (some texts list this as Senate whip) has the same duties as House majority whip.
- Committee chairpersons are from the majority party, usually assigned through seniority. As in House committees, the chairperson can wield power over when bills are debated, how they are debated, and sometimes even whether or not they are debated.
- A minority leader leads the interests of the minority party.
- A minority assistant (Senate whip) has duties like those of the House whips.
- Each party has a "Conference Caucus" that guides policies and agendas.

THE BASIC STEPS OF CREATING LAWS

The Constitution requires that revenue bills start in the House, but most bills are given simultaneous treatment by the House and Senate. Some bills are processed by the Senate and then the House, others by the House and then the Senate. All bills must be considered and approved by both chambers of Congress in order to become law.

Traditional committee procedures for debates, amendments, and votes have been modified by Congress to allow for more efficiency. Here are examples:

- **Fast tracking**—No amendments allowed; take the bill as is, or not at all. Because amendments are often lengthy and difficult to debate, fast tracking speeds the entire process.

- **Slow tracking**—Sequential committee hearings are required; this is usually a sign of a bill's being delayed through lengthier processing.

- **Multiple referrals**—Many bills need to be seen by different committees that cover areas of government under their control. To speed this process, bills can be sent to these committees simultaneously.

- **Outside amendments**—Some revisions can be set up by leaders to be added outside of committee meetings.

- **Unanimous consent rules**—As an efficiency measure, such rules allow for the usual procedures of votes to be suspended, as long as no single member objects. Long vote counts can be avoided.

- **King of the Hill votes**—This newer procedure has several amendment versions voted on in order. As long as amendments pass, the voting continues. When an amendment fails, the last one to win becomes the version selected for the bill. Prior amendments are then ignored.

- **Queen of the Hill votes**—This system gives the amendment with the biggest margin of approval the victory over all other amendments.

Legislation can be blocked in a variety of ways. Leaders can assign bills to openly hostile committees or committee chairpersons; chairpersons can delay the bill's consideration ("pigeonhole"); subcommittee and committee members can vote no (this is done often); subcommittee and committee amendments can change the bill so much that the original sponsors withdraw their support; lobby groups can create pressure to kill the bill; debate rules and issues can cause changes in votes or amendments; members of the Senate can filibuster or threaten to filibuster (senators can hold the floor as long as they can stand, thus delaying any other business; this tactic of "filibuster" can force compromises when the minority cannot stop a vote in any other manner); individual senators can place a "hold" on any bill and keep it from being debated on the floor; floor votes in either chamber can be no; the Conference Committee can change the bill enough to change support in chambers; and the president can pocket veto or veto (and Congress isn't able to override that veto).

Key Committees of Congress

House Committees:
Appropriations
Budget
Rules
Ways and Means

Senate Committees:
Appropriations
Budget
Finance
Foreign Relations
Judiciary

A Sample of Congressional Efficiency (Data from the 102nd Congress)

- Total bills introduced in the two-year term: 10,238 (100%)
- Bills sent to committees by leaders: 10,178 (99.4%)
- Bills referred out of committees: 1,205 (11.7%)
- Bills referred from floor debates: 1,201 (11.7%)
- Passed by both the House and the Senate: 667 (6.5%)
- Finally becoming federal law: 590 (5.7%) of all bills introduced

Opinions of Congress

Throughout recent history, citizens of the United States have had a split opinion about the members of Congress. As a branch, the vast majority of citizens hold negative opinions about the leaders and about their effectiveness. We don't trust Congress; we see the members as listening only to wealthy insiders and caring only for personal power. We believe that they are disconnected from the needs of the average citizen.

Yet, when polled about the work of our local representatives, opinions turn positive. Below are a few samples of major laws created by Congress (common names):

- Social Security Act 1935: New Deal safety net effort
- National Security Act 1947: Creation of Department of Defense, CIA, NSC
- Clean Air Act 1963: Antismog efforts start
- Civil Rights Act 1964: Racial discrimination outlawed
- Voting Rights Act 1965: Voting discrimination outlawed
- Freedom of Information Act 1966: Open records and fewer secrets mandated
- Fair Housing Act 1968: No housing discrimination
- Endangered Species Act 1973: Protects threatened species
- Americans with Disabilities Act 1991: Access for those with disabilities
- Family and Medical Leave Act 1993: Maternity and sick leave protection
- PATRIOT Act 2001: Department of Homeland Security created (post 9/11)
- No Child Left Behind Act 2001: Federal standards, rules, money in schools
- McCain-Feingold Act 2002: Efforts at "soft money" reform
- Sarbanes-Oaxley Act 2002: Corporate records need to be reliable
- American Jobs Creation Act 2004: Restructuring of business taxes
- Energy Independence and Security Act 2007: Focusing on renewable energy

❯❯ II. THE EXECUTIVE BRANCH

The President

The power and role of the U.S. president have greatly changed over the years. The original plan was for the executive officer to react to congressional laws and monitor their implementation, to represent the nation in foreign negotiations, and to suggest a list of national priorities. The Founding Fathers did not trust a single, powerful leader and made almost all the powers contingent on congressional involvement. In modern times, presidents hold significantly more powerful roles than they did years ago. Crises have demanded it, the public has wanted it, and Congress was unable (or unwilling) to stop it. Here are some examples:

- Lincoln suspended basic civil liberties during the chaos of 1861, when Congress couldn't even gather to act.
- Teddy Roosevelt sent the fleet into Asian conflicts and dared Congress to find the funding to bring it home.
- Franklin Roosevelt's staff began economic policies without congressional approval, and the nation demanded supportive action.

Recent presidents have sent troops into serious and violent conflicts without any declaration of war by Congress. The nation does not always have time to wait for a debate and majority vote.

At the president's disposal is a huge bureaucracy. Millions of employees and hundreds of agencies must answer to executive orders and directives. The president has a large, talented, and extremely loyal staff that can conduct research, give advice, and shield their leader.

Not every issue goes the way the president would like. As the center of media attention, a president often takes blame for activities beyond his or her control. Congress is happy to spread that blame, even if items such as taxes and budgets are actually its responsibility.

QUALIFICATIONS: FORMAL AND INFORMAL

The founders included no requirement of experience, education, or skills. The only requirements that were listed were as follows:

- A set age (at least 35 years old)
- Citizenship (natural born)
- Residency (14 years in the United States)

It was expected that the electoral college would be careful in selecting only the most qualified individuals. Modern politics and elections make it clear that parties and citizens prefer candidates with strong party agendas, personal wealth, images of decisive leadership, and good television presentation skills.

Informal Qualifications of the Presidency

Historically, citizens have chosen certain kinds of leaders for the presidency. Clearly, trends change, but to date, here's a generalization of the major features of our presidents:

- Male
- European American (In 2009, Barack Obama was the first African American to become president.)
- Middle-aged
- Wealthy
- Protestant (Kennedy's candidacy as a Roman Catholic was questioned.)
- College graduate

- Healthy
- Married (All presidents [except Buchanan] have been married.)
- Has leadership or military skills
- Is from an important electoral state (Notable exception: Bill Clinton from Arkansas)
- Debates well (Post-1960, the TV image has been emphasized.)

STAFF INFLUENCES

Upon attaining office, a president is supported and at times controlled by powerful staff structures. The vice president can influence many decisions through congressional contacts. The chief of staff can screen access to the president and filter information available to him or her. The press secretary plays the role of selecting how messages are delivered from the office to the media.

Economic and military experts guide the president in areas of policy. The Cabinet controls the daily workings of large parts of the executive bureaucracy and is in charge of suggesting candidates for most of the 5,000 jobs the president is expected to appoint.

IMPORTANT INFORMAL DUTIES

The president fulfills a critical advisory role. He is the leader of his party, supporting candidates and the party platform. He is the national focal point during times of emergency and crisis. He works face-to-face with international leaders, representing the goals of the nation.

THE POWER OF EXECUTIVE PRIVILEGE

Presidents have used the concept of separation of powers to claim a status above the scrutiny of Congress or the courts. As leader, a president can claim that certain decisions, information, documents, and secrets of executive agencies are the private business of the president, the president's staff, and the military.

The most famous dispute in this area was the Watergate tapes of Richard Nixon. When Congress pressed for those tapes as part of a potential criminal investigation, Nixon refused to turn them over. He claimed that they were personal documents for his own use in creating memoirs. The Supreme Court had to step in and resolve the dispute on behalf of Congress. Presidents cannot hide behind executive privilege to put themselves above the reach of the law.

Constitutional Duties and Powers of the President (Article 2 and Article 4, Section 4)

Duties and Powers	Constraints
• Serves as commander-in-chief of the military (national security leader).	• Congress funds and organizes the military and makes the rules of the military.
• Negotiates treaties with foreign governments (foreign policy leader).	• The Senate must approve treaties for them to take effect.
• Nominates top federal officials, including federal judges and justices of the Supreme Court.	• The Senate must approve the nominations and, by tradition, "Senatorial courtesy" is often expected for nominations.
• Vetoes legislation passed by Congress.	• Congress can override the veto with a two-thirds vote in both chambers.
• Can use a pocket veto.	• No constraints exist if the president does not sign legislation passed with fewer than 10 days left in the session.
• Faithfully administers federal laws (national policy leader); uses orders, proclamations, and memoranda.	• Congress has set up its own agencies to counter executive priorities (Congressional Budget Office versus the White House's Office of Management and Budget) and has given many powers to independent agencies.
• Can pardon people.	• Public outrage may imperil popularity and re-election chances (e.g., Gerald Ford's pardon of Nixon).
• Addresses Congress and the nation and sets the priorities of the legislation (State of the Union message; legislative leader).	• Congress can ignore the priorities, especially if gridlock exists between the branches.

There are different types of presidential directives to the executive branch:

- An executive order has the force of law and is listed in the *Federal Register*. It can affect millions of federal workers and all agencies. Such an order is a very powerful policy tool.

- Many environmental policies and civil rights policies, such as affirmative action, began as executive orders to the bureaucracy.

- A proclamation is often merely a ceremonial action and is not law.

- Memoranda are issued to specific agencies, usually for single projects, but they can affect the way that agency conducts business.

EXPANSION OF PRESIDENTIAL POWERS

- 1845 (Polk): As commander-in-chief, Polk ordered the army into disputed territories claimed by Mexico, thus starting battles without Congress's permission or a declaration of war.

- 1861 (Lincoln): Lincoln declared a domestic emergency during a congressional recess, changing the way a president can act during a crisis. Lincoln also suspended habeas corpus rights.

- Early 1900s (T. Roosevelt): Roosevelt pushed the public to demand economic reforms, used the press as his agenda vehicle, and even sent the U.S. Navy on a mission without congressional funds or approval.

- 1930s (F. D. Roosevelt): As head of the executive branch, FDR created federal economic programs and reorganized the executive branch—without prior congressional approval. The resulting challenges put Congress in a position of reaction, not creation. When the Supreme Court started to halt New Deal programs, FDR hit it with a "packing" plan that failed, but he forced court retirements and changed the court's reaction to public pressure.

- Late 1960s (Nixon): Nixon blocked congressional programs by "impounding" funds for programs he didn't support. Congress was forced to legislate changes in the spending of program monies. The Supreme Court supported Congress.

- Early 1980s (Reagan): Through the Office of Management and Budget, Reagan's director, David Stockman, attacked programs by eliminating them from the budget. Congress had to go into a reaction mode again to attempt some restoration of programs.

- Modern times (several): The power of the executive order has increased over time. By ordering the huge bureaucracy to follow specific orders about certain programs or the spending of funds, the president can effect sweeping changes in the government and economy.

Recent Trends

Increased use of committee powers: Senate committees, such as the Foreign Relations Committee, have increased their activities against presidential nominations. Famous examples include Senator Jesse Helms's blocks of Clinton nominees and threats of filibusters over conservative judges by Democratic senators in 2005.

Increasing use of "independent counsels": Investigative committees have led to growing congressional attacks on presidents. Examples include Watergate, Iran-Contra, Whitewater, and the Clinton impeachment.

Evidence of presidential "success" as of the election of 2008: In 18 elections, the incumbent president was successful in getting re-elected. In 19 elections, he was not. This does not include elections where former presidents were unable even to be named as their party's candidate.

❯ III. THE FEDERAL BUREAUCRACY

The Fourth Branch

One of the biggest changes in government structure has been the development of vast networks of agencies and departments that make up the "fourth branch." In early decades, presidents had a few key officials run small departments that handled a few embassies, created some banks and currency, worked with military leaders, and built the postal system. This eventually led to a civil service organization of qualified professionals, which now includes 15 departments and over 150 regulatory agencies.

Scope of Powers

The federal bureaucracy has two central powers: rule making and rule adjudication. When agencies are asked to create rules that will govern their actions, they are completing a form of legislative power. Agencies often announce the creation of rules and hold public hearings to allow for input, but once the rules are finalized, the public has to abide by their structure. Agencies such as OSHA (Occupational Safety and Health Administration) have a great deal of authority over business actions and can punish businesses severely for breaking codes.

CONTROLS ON BUREAUCRACY

The bureaucracy is not without outside controls. The president and the Office of Management and Budget control agencies' budget access. If no budget resources are assigned, then the agency loses power. Congress can also change budget priorities and send in the General Accounting Office to hold lengthy audits, checking the propriety of an agency's spending.

Basics of the Bureaucracy

Bureaucracies grow during economic crises and in periods of war. Because of regulations and the numerous jobs created, bureaucracies are very difficult to remove or reduce once established. About 3 million people work for the federal government. This is economically very significant to many communities and states.

Because Congress does not have the time or expertise to run the complex government on a day-to-day basis, permanent bureaucracies are able to put forward reasonable solutions. Bureaucratic leaders are experts in science and other disciplines, and that gives them high levels of influence. Bureaucracy rules are complex and give those in the agencies a great deal of leverage in carrying out these rules.

The Powerful Iron Triangles of Policy

Agencies are a key part of political power known as "iron triangles of power." Iron triangles is a term used to describe the policy-making relationship among congressional committees, the bureaucracy, and interest groups. A famous example is tobacco subsidies. They are supported by legislators from states where the crop is grown, large cigarette lobbies, and the Department of Agriculture. The department needs the funds to monitor and control, the lobbies love the profits, and the politicians love the campaign funds. This relationship creates a three-way, stable alliance that is sometimes called a *subgovernment* because of its durability, impregnability, and power to determine policy.

The Major Units of the Bureaucracy

The Executive Branch

- **Executive Office of the President (EOP):** Consists of the agencies and individuals who directly help the President and includes the following:
- **Vice President's Office (VP)**
- **White House Office (WHO):** The daily staff of the president ("West Wing")
- **Council of Economic Advisors (CEA):** Three economic policy experts
- **National Security Council (NSC):** VP, Secretary of Defense, Secretary of State, leaders of the Joint Chiefs, CIA Director, NSC Advisor
- **Office of Management and Budget (OMB):** Creating the federal budget
- **U.S. Trade Representative (USTR):** Policy with groups such as the World Trade Organization
- **Cabinet:** 15 departments (Includes State Department and Homeland Security.) As close advisors to the President, cabinet members can wield considerable power.

The Legislative Branch

- **Congressional Budget Office (CBO):** Congress's fiscal policy experts
- **General Accounting Office (GAO):** Congress's agency that monitors the spending of federal funds
- **Library of Congress (LOC):** The national library and data system

Major Independent Agencies Duty Areas

- **Consumer Product Safety Commission (CPSC):** Product warnings, recalls
- **Environmental Protection Agency (EPA):** Air, land, water
- **Equal Employment Opportunity Commission (EEOC):** Fairness in the workplace
- **Federal Reserve (FED):** National banking and U.S. bond markets, interest rates
- **Federal Emergency Management Agency (FEMA):** Federal disaster relief
- **National Aeronautics and Space Administration (NASA):** Federal space research
- **National Endowment for the Arts (NEA):** Funds for public arts
- **National Science Foundation (NSF):** Grants for research to universities and labs
- **Nuclear Regulatory Commission (NRC):** Domestic power from nuclear fission
- **Peace Corps:** International assistance
- **Securities and Exchange Commission (SEC):** Regulating stocks and bond markets
- **Smithsonian Institute:** National museums and their collections

COMPONENTS OF IRON TRIANGLES

1. Members of Congress whose districts/states benefit financially from programs will vote to keep them in the budget.
2. Lobby and interest groups that get support and influence from the programs will transfer that support into campaign funds, influence peddling, and letter drives.
3. The federal agencies that benefit from running and monitoring the programs need the programs in order to have something to control.

WHY IRON TRIANGLES ARE SO POWERFUL

- Government issues are now so vast and complex that smaller governmental units find themselves independent and very much in charge of local and regional policies.
- All three of the main groups that control the triangles benefit from keeping the programs in place, whether or not the public or other agencies see the need.
- Members of Congress get more campaign funds, more name recognition in the district, and more credit for jobs and money.
- Lobby and interest groups keep their supporters in power and keep their contracts, jobs, and benefits.
- Federal agencies have more reasons to exist.

❯❯ IV. THE JUDICIAL SYSTEM AND CIVIL LIBERTIES

Introduction

Legal issues in the United States are classified in two ways. Civil law covers relations between individuals and defines their rights. Criminal law covers illegal actions or wrongful acts and can result in fines, imprisonment, and possibly even the death sentence.

When courts rule, they use four kinds of law. The first is *common law,* which is derived from precedents set by courts of the past. Common law traditions can extend back to rights established in colonial, English, and some French courts (Louisiana). When legislative bodies create laws, these codes become *statutory law.* Because the public elects the representatives who create statutory law, courts consider it more compelling than common law. When agencies create rules and rulings that concern their areas of influence, these become *administrative law. Constitutional law* covers the broad area of interpretation under judicial review.

Two-Court System

The court structure of the United States remains one of the best examples of the federal system. States have unique legal traditions, handle most civil and criminal cases that occur in the country, and have separate systems for appeals from lower courts. The states' jurisdictions have always been given the label *general law.*

Federal courts work within the boundaries of federal law—cases that are "limited and exclusive jurisdiction" go to federal courts. Only those cases arising from interstate issues, conflicts with federal authorities, issues specific to sections of the Bill of Rights, and crimes listed as federal in nature by Congress are heard in federal courts. The Supreme Court has ruled in many cases to expand federal authority, but such expansions only occur after specific legal challenges. States continue to hold rule over most legal activities in the country.

BASICS OF THE DUAL COURT SYSTEM

The following fall under "general law and jurisdiction" of the United States:

- Most civil disputes between citizens are settled in state civil courts.
- Most criminal disputes in the United States are settled in state criminal courts.
- Appeals from state courts are sent to state appeals court systems. Such appeals may end in state supreme courts.

The following fall under "limited and exclusive jurisdiction" of federal law:

- Federal civil disputes are heard in specific federal courts or federal district courts.
- Federal criminal cases are usually heard in federal district courts.
- Examples of federal "limited and exclusive jurisdiction" from the Constitution or laws passed by Congress include these: counterfeiting of U.S. currency; kidnapping; mail fraud; interstate trade conflicts; national banking conflicts; conflicts with federal agencies; U.S. border issues; RICO crimes (racketeering); civil right conflicts; and conflicts over patents, copyrights, and customs rulings.

LAYERS OF DUAL COURTS

Both the states and the federal court systems consist of layers of courts. At the federal level, most cases begin in district courts, which are found in most urban centers. If appeals are granted, cases move to regional courts of appeals or circuit courts. There are 12 such courts of appeals.

Creation of Judicial Review

The single most significant change in judicial history was the creation of the power of judicial review. The Supreme Court used the 1803 decision in *Marbury v. Madison* to establish this authority.

William Marbury headed a list of Federalist appointees that claimed that Jefferson and his Secretary of State James Madison were hiding their appointment papers. Marbury demanded that the Court force the delivery of the papers by using a law that Congress had created, giving the Supreme Court the power to make the ruling. Chief Justice John Marshall ruled that the law that gave them such powers was itself unconstitutional and, therefore, they couldn't give the order to the president. Judicial review gives the Supreme Court the power to decide the constitutionality of laws and other actions of the government.

The "Second" Constitution

Within the dual court system, the greatest change has been the use of the 14th Amendment to apply many sections of the Bill of Rights to state laws. The 14th Amendment contains language that requires all states to give all citizens due process and equal protection.

Case decisions in the 20th century caused interpretations where specific rights in the other amendments applied to states through the 14th Amendment's requirements. This development is now known as the Incorporation Doctrine. Now states must, in their own courts and laws, give citizens protections such as rights to counsel and rights for limited search, seizure, or arrest.

RIGHTS IN THE BILL OF RIGHTS THAT HAVE BEEN "INCORPORATED" THROUGH THE 14TH AMENDMENT VIA SUPREME COURT RULINGS

(Note that not all of the rights listed in the Bill of Rights have been "incorporated," because some of the rights have not been challenged in cases or have not been accepted for such challenges by the Supreme Court.)

- Privacy (not listed in the Bill of Rights but implied and interpreted from several amendment cases)
- Free speech (First Amendment)
- Free press (First Amendment)
- Freedom of religion (First Amendment)
- Assembly and petition rights (First Amendment)

- "Association" (First Amendment)
- Search and seizure (Fourth Amendment)
- "Exclusion" of evidence (implied in cases dealing with the Fourth Amendment, such as *Mapp v. Ohio*)
- Self-incrimination (Sixth Amendment)
- Confront witnesses (Sixth Amendment)
- Impartial jury (Sixth Amendment)
- Speedy trial (Sixth Amendment)
- Right to counsel (Sixth Amendment)
- Public trial (Sixth Amendment)
- Cruel and unusual punishment (Eighth Amendment)

Structure of the Federal Court System

LOWER FEDERAL COURTS (TRIAL COURTS WHERE JURIES MAY BE PRESENT; RUN BY FEDERAL JUDGES)

- U.S. District Courts (94 across the country as of 2010)
- Various military courts and tribunals
- Courts, hearings, panels of various federal agencies, including independent agencies
- Bankruptcy Courts (officially they are units of the District Courts)
- U.S. Court of Federal Claims (claims against the United States; 16 judges run this court)
- U.S. Court of International Trade
- U.S. Tax Court
- Courts of the District of Columbia
- U.S. Territorial Courts (Guam, Northern Mariana Islands, U.S. Virgin Islands)
- Foreign Intelligence Surveillance Court

APPEALS COURTS (ALSO RUN BY FEDERAL JUDGES)

- Legislative Appeals Courts
- U.S. Court of Appeals for the Armed Services
- U.S. Court of Appeals for the Federal Circuit
- The U.S. Courts of Appeals (13 circuits, including D.C., 6 to 28 judges in each; these 13 courts hear appeals from the Federal District Courts)

THE SUPREME COURT

- Nine federal justices (The number is set by Congress.)
- Original jurisdiction cases cover foreign diplomats, United States versus a state, a state versus another state, a state versus citizens of another state, a state versus a foreign country.
- Appellate jurisdiction covers cases granted from U.S. courts of appeals, state supreme courts, the U.S. Court of Appeals for the Armed Services, and the Court of Appeals for the Federal Circuit.
- The vast majority of cases appealed to the Supreme Court under writs of certiorari are denied hearings by the Supreme Court justices. Thousands of requests are made annually, but the Supreme Court will hear only about 100 cases. Those cases not granted hearings are returned (remanded) to the last court, where that decision stands.

JUDICIAL TERMS

Supreme Court justices can serve for life terms. This makes their initial selection important and very political. Members of the Supreme Court are expected by liberals and conservatives to express strong political viewpoints on the uses of the Constitution. The spectrum of opinions forms around the issue of the powers of government, just like the sides taken by parties.

Once a nomination is sent by the president, the Senate Judiciary Committee plays the key role of supporting or opposing the judge's political bias. Those who favor a more open interpretation of the powers of the Constitution are labeled judicial liberals, and those who oppose that view are judicial conservatives.

The Supreme Court's Work

Justices of the Supreme Court must be nominated by the president and approved by the Senate. The vast majority (99 percent) of cases appealed to the court are remanded, making the lower court's decision final.

The Supreme Court functions in a very egalitarian manner. The chief justice is a guide and meeting chairperson but has no special voting powers. The chief does not have to be part of the majority. Conferences and debates in the court have traditionally been relatively secret events, with books and memoirs being published only recently revealing how decisions are argued or finalized. Attorneys are very limited in their presentations, and any member of the court can ask any question he or she considers important.

FUNCTIONS OF THE SUPREME COURT

Once the court has a majority of five to nine justices, it can explain to the legal community what it wants the decision to mean for the law. The majority opinion becomes the guide to interpreting the decision's effect on the use of the Constitution. If one to four justices disagree with the ruling, the court can publish a minority opinion explaining those opinions. Minority opinions are often used by the legal community for future challenges.

THE CHIEF JUSTICE'S ROLE

Courts are named after the chief justice. For example, the current Supreme Court is headed by Chief Justice John Roberts and is referred to as the Roberts Court. The chief organizes meetings and guides discussions, but all other justices have equal votes.

There have been 17 chief justices under 44 U.S. presidents. The following four are possibly the most famous and represent significant court eras and changes:

- John Marshall   1801–1835   34 years   Helped found many early court powers
- Roger Taney   1836–1864   28 years   Dominated mid-1800s and Civil War
- Earl Warren   1953–1969   16 years   Major civil rights changes and cases
- William Rehnquist   1986–2005   19 years   Major conservative influence

THE IMPORTANCE OF COURT RULINGS

Supreme Court rulings are central to understanding the development of civil rights and civil liberties in the United States. Civil rights stem from the Declaration of Independence statement that "all men are created equal," rights given by the "equal protection" section of the 14th Amendment, and laws from Congress. They cover issues such as racial discrimination, voting rights, and privacy. Civil liberties cover the freedoms that citizens have from governmental interference and control. Many civil liberties were incorporated under the due process section of the 14th Amendment as it applies to the other portions of the Bill of Rights. Courts have used different legal tests to determine which groups can claim which kinds of rights. Courts have determined that women are a minority group due to persistent historic forms of discrimination. Minority status also applies to ethnic minorities and to people with certain disabilities.

Civil Liberties and Equal Protection

Categories of people who are considered for equal protection include the following:

- Age groups
- Racial classification groups
- Gender groups
- Economic status groups

The Judiciary and the Political Spectrum

Justices and judges have political interests and agendas. Federal judges try to build a legacy of political bias to improve their standing for advancement under Republican or Democratic administrations. The selection of Supreme Court justices has always been a game of maneuvering for liberal, conservative, or moderate ideals. The history of presidents and judicial appointments has been a history of selections for the "correct" biases. Recent famous examples include Eisenhower's disappointment with Earl Warren's liberalism, the Senate's rejection of Reagan's conservative nominee Robert Bork, and Antonin Scalia's rise as the conservative standard on the court.

Presidents have a long and consistent record of selecting an overwhelming number of judges and justices with political beliefs similar to their own. Members of the courts tend to follow the biases of the major parties, with the additional consideration of broad or limited interpretations of the Constitution. Justices who hesitate to strike down laws unless they are obviously unconstitutional are said to be exercising judicial restraint, while those who rulings are suspected of being based on personal convictions or political considerations rather than on existing law are said to be exercising judicial activism.

KINDS OF JUDICIAL BIASES/VIEWPOINTS

Judicial liberals tend to support the following:

- Broad interpretations of the Elastic Clause ("necessary and proper")
- Broad interpretations of civil rights acts and laws
- Pro-choice decisions
- Strict limits on the separation of church and state (no school prayer)
- Affirmative action programs to end discrimination

Judicial conservatives tend to support the following:

- Stricter limits on the use of the Commerce Clause (less power for feds)
- Limited uses of "necessary and proper" in context of Article 1, Section 8
- More local and state control of civil rights questions
- Community standards for speech and obscenity
- Affirmative action as a form of reverse discrimination

Some of the Most Famous Court Cases

Precedent-setting court cases are the focus of much study and memorization. They have been used to create a list of legal interpretations, limits on police powers, limits on citizens' rights, and limits on governmental actions. These cases summarize the various interpretations of key rights such as speech, religion, and search and seizure. The following table attempts to present those cases likely to be mentioned in AP exams.

- *Marbury v. Madison,* **1803:** Judicial review established.

- *McCulloch v. Maryland,* **1819:** Federal "implied powers" exapanded; federal banks allowed.

- *Gibbons v. Ogden,* **1824:** Commerce Clause gives Congress broad powers to regulate interstate commerce.

- *Dred Scott v. Sanford,* **1857:** African Americans are not citizens but property.

- *Munn v. Illinois,* **1876:** States can regulate privately owned businesses in the public's interest.

- *Plessy v. Ferguson,* **1896:** "Separate but Equal" facilities for African Americans are constitutional.

- *Schenk v. United States,* **1919:** "Clear and Present Danger Test" to limit speech.

- *Gitlow v. New York,* **1925:** Limits on "anarchy," but free speech "incorporated."

- *Near v. Minnesota,* **1931:** No "prior restraint" of the freedom of the press.

- *Korematsu v. United States,* **1944:** Government can intern (detain) citizens in emergencies.

- *Brown v. Board of Education,* **1954:** Overturned *Plessy* in public schools.

- *Roth v. United States,* **1957:** Obscenity is not free speech.

- *Mapp v. Ohio,* **1961:** Warrants needed for evidence to be used (exclusion).

- *Baker v. Carr,* **1962:** State apportionment must be "one man = one vote."

- *Engel v. Vitale,* **1962:** No school-led daily prayer in public schools.

- *Gideon v. Wainright,* **1963:** States must provide attorneys in state courts.

- *Heart of Atlanta v. United States,* **1964:** Commerce Clause applies to private business/interstate activities.

- *Griswold v. Connecticut,* **1965:** Information about birth control is a privacy right.

- *Miranda v. Arizona,* **1966:** Police must explain rights at the time of arrest.

- *Terry v. Ohio,* **1968:** Police can search and seize with probable cause.

- *Lemon v. Kurtzman,* **1971:** Some government aid to church schools is allowed (Lemon Test).

- *New York Times Co. v. United States,* **1971:** No prior restraint of the stolen Pentagon Papers.

- *Miller v. California,* **1973:** Community standards determine obscenity.

- *Roe v. Wade,* **1973:** First trimester abortions legal due to medical privacy.

- *United States v. Nixon,* **1974:** Executive privilege does not extend to criminal cases.

- *Gregg v. Georgia,* **1976:** Death penalty upheld within the Eighth Amendment.

- *Buckley v. Valeo,* **1976:** Campaign money limits, but independent and personal money allowed.

- *Regents v. Bakke,* **1978:** No racial quotas allowed, but race can be considered.

- *New Jersey v. T.L.O.,* **1985:** School searches without warrants possible.

- *Hazelwood v. Kuhlmeier,* **1988:** School newspapers can be censored by teachers, administrators.

- *Texas v. Johnson,* **1989:** Flag burning is a form of political free speech.

- *Planned Parenthood v. Casey,* **1992:** States can put some restrictions on *Roe* rights.

- *Santa Fe ISD v. Doe,* **2000:** No school-led prayers at extracurricular events.

- *Gratz v. Bollinger,* **2003:** Affirmative action at colleges okay but limited.

Believers in *judicial activism* (policy activism; structural activism; also known as broad constructionism or loose constructionism) tend to support the following:

- Overturning previous cases readily if those are seen as wrong
- Judicial review as a proper and well-established power
- The 14th Amendment giving the federal government power to "incorporate"
- The idea that the history of state and local courts is a history of abuses of civil rights and segregation and the federal government should step in
- The idea that the Constitution is silent on rights like "privacy" and "innocent until proven guilty," so the courts can protect these broadly
- The idea that the Founding Fathers expected leaders to adapt the Constitution over time and wrote the document with this in mind
- The idea that courts might try to correct laws, institutions, or state controls over issues such as search and seizure rights, privacy rights, and counsel rights (These are often seen as pro-liberal in bias.)

Believers in *judicial restraint* (also known as strict constructionism or original intent) tend to support the following:

- Not overturning previous cases if possible
- Natural rights of citizens that government must leave alone
- Article 3 as a statement of Supreme Court powers to resolve disputes only
- Article 3 as not giving the Supreme Court the right to "create" policy
- The 9th and 10th Amendments, leaving rights to citizens and states
- The idea that Congress should be in charge of new policy or create amendments
- The idea that proper state authority should be emphasized
- The idea that the Founding Fathers built a government of limits and these should be followed

Practice Section

› FREE-RESPONSE QUESTIONS

1. The idea of "necessary and proper" powers has been used to expand the scope of Congress's authority.

   (A) Identify the political name of the use of these powers.

   (B) Identify the power listed in Article 1 of the Constitution that Congress has most often expanded.

   (C) Identify and describe how one of the following cases was used for expansion of powers:

   Gibbons v. Ogden, 1824
   Heart of Atlanta Motel v. U.S., 1964

2. Congress has created a system of lawmaking that is slow, difficult, and usually kills bills.

   (A) List and explain two ways Congress stops legislation.

   (B) Explain two reasons why this might be intentional and beneficial.

3. Though the founders intended Congress to be the supreme federal branch, presidents now find themselves the center of more attention and power.

   (A) Identify and describe two ways this trend toward presidential power has occurred (not counting the presidential authority over the bureaucracy).

   (B) Identify and explain how presidential authority over the federal bureaucracy has increased executive powers.

4. Recent Congresses have attempted to regain authority from presidents.

   (A) Identify and describe at least two such efforts by Congress.

   (B) Identify and describe one way Congress has failed in these efforts.

5. The federal bureaucracy has gained power within the federal system.

   (A) Identify and explain a "legislative" power assumed by the bureaucracy.

   (B) Identify and explain an "executive" power assumed by the bureaucracy.

   (C) Identify and explain a "judicial" power assumed by the bureaucracy.

6. Many see the federal bureaucracy as growing too rapidly and gaining too much power.

   (A) Identify how each of the three branches of the federal government can attempt to control the bureaucracy.

   (B) Explain at least one option the general public has in controlling bureaucratic powers.

7. The judicial system of the United States is still the most "federal" part of the government.

   (A) Define how the court system is "federal" in structure.

   (B) Identify three kinds of authority federal courts control and what this overall level of power is called.

   (C) Identify two kinds of authority state courts control and what this overall level of power is called.

8. Cases can reach the Supreme Court in two main ways.

   (A) Define the two ways cases go to the Supreme Court.

   (B) Identify two kinds of cases that go directly to the Supreme Court.

   (C) Identify at least two steps that occur when cases are appealed and accepted by the Supreme Court.

Answers and Explanations

1. **4-point Rubric**

   1 point in part (A): (identify)

   - Elastic Clause

   1 point in part (B): (identify)

   - Commerce Clause
   - Regulation of interstate commerce

   2 points in part (C): (identify issue/describe)

   - *Gibbons v. Ogden*, 1824—Conflicts over the control of interstate trade are in the hands of Congress. They are not in the hands of the states. Licenses across state boundaries fall within the commerce powers of Congress.
   - *Heart of Atlanta Motel v. United* States, 1964—Civil rights requirements from the federal government (acts of Congress) apply to private businesses if they conduct interstate trade activities or benefit substantially from interstate trade.

2. **6-point Rubric**

   4 points in part (A): (identify and explain)

   - Chairperson or subcommittee chairperson—pigeonhole or delay bill to death.
   - Subcommittee or committee—vote bill down.
   - Floor debate—vote bill down.
   - Other chamber—vote bill down at some step.
   - President—veto or pocket veto and bill dies.
   - Congress—no override vote.

   2 points in part (B): (reasons this might be positive)

   - Deliberation is good.
   - Majority consensus is needed.
   - Emotional responses need time to be considered.
   - Consensus from multiple branches shows need.
   - Plenty of points of access by the public, lobby forces, or other leaders.

3. **6-point Rubric**

   4 points in part (A): (identify and describe evidence of trend toward president)

   - Military initiative; Polk's placing troops in conflict and forcing Congress to act.
   - Emergency initiative; Lincoln's suspension of writ of habeas corpus rights during the emergency of 1861.
   - Economic initiative; FDR's creation of offices and agencies to help during the Great Depression crisis.
   - Deregulation initiative; Carter's starting the trend of cutting federal involvement (other examples of this nature would work).

   2 points in part (B): (identify and explain power over the bureaucracy)

   - Executive orders; power of law to require actions of the agencies.
   - Executive memoranda; power of actions over certain agencies.

4. **6-point Rubric**

   4 points in part (A): (identify and describe efforts by Congress)

   - Limit military powers; take back control of troops in conflict.
   - Restrict budget powers; force presidents to spend money.
   - Appointments; restrict and investigate appointments more.
   - Investigate; openly attack presidential behaviors.
   - Budget fights; try to force policies by not passing budgets.

   2 points in part (B): (identify and describe failures by Congress)

   - Gingrich budget fights; public ended up blaming Congress.
   - Impeachment; Clinton scandals don't lead to removal.
   - Crisis; powers go back to president after 9/11.
   - Division; Congress continues to be split, with many supporting the president.

5. **6-point Rubric**

   2 points for each identify and explain in (A), (B), (C)

   - Legislative: Agencies must create the rules and regulations needed to enact their duties, because Congress doesn't have the time or expertise.
   - Executive: Agencies put general rules into effect, often after they have had the duty to create the very rules they execute.
   - Judicial: Agencies rule on licenses, access, and activities allowed for businesses and individuals, with penalties and fines possible.
   - Congress does not have time.
   - Congress doesn't have the expertise.
   - The president does not have time.
   - The court system can't handle all possible agency problems.

6. **4-point Rubric**

   3 points in part (A): (identify how branches can control the bureaucracy)

   - Legislative: Controls the budgets, creates new rules/restrictions, and can cut agency.
   - Executive: Orders and memoranda direct agencies to follow presidential directives.
   - Judicial: If challenges are brought, the agency actions can be cut down, overturned, and eliminated.

   1 point in part (B): (public controls)

   - Lobby Congress.
   - Lobby the agency directly.
   - Challenge agency in court.

7. **8-point Rubric**

   1 point in part (A): (define)

   - Dual court system: Two distinct levels of jurisdiction, strong state involvement.

   4 points in part (B): (three kinds of federal, label)

   - "Limited and exclusive jurisdiction."
   - Federal civil law.
   - Federal criminal law.
   - Federal appeals.
   - Constitutional jurisdiction counterfeiting, interstate conflicts, state versus state.
   - Crimes made federal, kidnapping, civil rights abuses, attacking federal officials.

   3 points in part (C): (two kinds of state authority, label)

   - "General law/general jurisdiction."
   - State civil laws.
   - State criminal codes.
   - State appeals.
   - Common law of state courts.
   - State statutory laws.

8. **6-point Rubric**

2 points in part (A): (two ways to the Supreme Court)

- Appeal from lower federal courts.
- Appeal from the highest state courts.
- Original jurisdiction cases.

2 points in part (B): (two cases that go directly to the Supreme Court)

- State versus state.
- Ambassadors and public ministers.

2 points in part (C): (two steps to acceptance)

- Submission of writ of certiorari.
- Rule of Four vote.

CHAPTER 4

Government Policies

❯ I. THE FEDERAL BUDGET AND ECONOMIC POLICIES

The Budget

Tax collections and budget expenditures now approach trillions of dollars annually. The federal budget process prioritizes where funds go and what can be done with them. The federal budget year, called the fiscal year, goes from October 1 through September 30. The Office of Management and Budget (OMB), under the executive branch, is responsible for drafting the budget. The Congressional Budget Office (CBO) is the professional staff group responsible for giving Congress budget projections and priorities and balancing the OMB's priorities with Congress's policy interests.

The Senate Appropriations Committee and the House Appropriations Committee are in charge of final budget numbers. Chairpersons of these committees are considered some of the most powerful leaders of Congress. Each committee has 12 subcommittees that deal with budget issues concerning the different parts of government (defense, energy, security, etc.). The chairpersons of the 24 subcommittees are known as the "Budget Cardinals" and have vast influence over program priorities. The main focus of the budget is on "discretionary" programs, which Congress can choose to fund. Mandatory programs are already set for funding. Congress has to authorize borrowing to cover funding.

Recent Budget Example of Revenues and Expenditures

Revenues and Sources = $1.946 Trillion

- Individual Income Tax Receipts 50%
- Social Security Taxes and Contributions 32%
- Corporate Income Tax Receipts 10%
- Federal Excise Taxes 3%
- Deposit on Federal Earnings 2%
- Estate, Gift Tax Receipts 1%
- Federal Customs, Duties, Tariff Receipts 1%

Expenditures and Sources = $2.052 Trillion

- Social Security Payments 22%
- Defense 16%
- Income Security 14%
- Net Interest Payments on the Public Debt 12%
- Medicare Payments 11%
- Health Payments 8%
- Veterans' Benefits 3%
- Education 3%
- All Other Spending on Programs 11% (running the government agencies, transportation funds, energy funds, court funds, etc.)

Creating the Budget—Needs and Priorities

Creating the budget takes three major policy steps: agenda building, policy formation, and policy adoption. At the center is the money needed to run any program or agency that will provide services or execute laws. Once programs are in place, further evaluation occurs to determine if programs work as intended or if they need modification. The Constitution requires that Congress, specifically the House, initiate the collecting and spending of revenues annually. The federal government cannot raise revenues without legislative action.

Congressional committees are central in the development of the budget. Membership on the Senate and House Appropriations Committees is seen as a key position of power over projects and political priorities. Subcommittee and committee chairpersons are some of the most influential people in Washington. Congress becomes a reactionary group, trying to figure out how the OMB has created priorities, dealing with biases, and then attempting to support or change them. Congressional leaders and committees must also try to add all of their "pork barrel" projects as amendments or separate pieces of legislation. To help with this monumental task and to attempt to balance some of the control of data by the OMB, Congress created the CBO, which guides the leaders of the legislature in setting priorities.

Budget Issues

Three major issues now dominate all discussions of budget and policy. The first is the growing obligation of Social Security. Because Social Security payments are funded by the tax contributions of current workers and the average life expectancy is increasing while the birthrate is decreasing, Social Security faces a long-term solvency problem.

The second issue is the massive government debt that has accumulated in record amounts since the 1980s. Hundreds of billions of dollars are now needed annually just to keep up with the interest payments on the various government bond promises. In recent years, the debate has become even more political as foreign governments, such as South Korea and the People's Republic of China, have purchased substantial sums of the bonds that finance the debt. Will future taxpayers be willing to see vast fortunes pass on to foreign governments? As more annual deficits add to the total debt, more interest payments are needed, further decreasing the amount available for discretionary needs.

The third controversy stems from key disagreements about the government's role in economic policies. Federal statutes require that the government must try to keep the economy stable and growing, but there is no consensus on how this is best done or even if the government should try. Interest rate policies, reactions to inflation, reactions to tax systems, and subsidy programs are expensive and may only be beneficial to some communities.

Economic Policy Terms and Theories

Supply-side policies: Supply-side theorists believe that the government should concentrate its efforts on increasing the supply of, not the demand for, goods and services. This theory maintains that tax cuts will give businesses and individuals more money to spend on establishing and expanding businesses, which will cause the economy to grow.

Keynesian policies: According to this theory, which is named after the British economist John Maynard Keynes, government should stimulate consumer demand for good and services. In times of depression or recession, the government should increase spending even if this requires borrowing money to do so. In times of inflation, the government should raise taxes to reduce the amount of money in circulation, thus lowering demand for goods and services.

Presidential Economic Programs

Trust Busting/Progressivism
T. Roosevelt
Early 1900s
These efforts were results of the late 1800s Populist upsurge and growing demands for industrial reforms.

New Deal
F. Roosevelt
1930s
Massive help from government programs was needed and translated into key social programs such as Social Security.

Fair Deal
H. Truman
Late 1940s
Efforts to preserve and extend the liberal policies of President Franklin Delano Roosevelt's New Deal.

Great Society
L. Johnson
Mid-1960s
Vast attempts were made to rebuild inner cities, create jobs, and provide financial assistance.

New Federalism
R. Nixon
Early 1970s
Policies that shifted money and power away from the federal bureaucracy and toward states and municipalities.

Whip Inflation Now (WIN)
G. Ford
Mid-1970s
More federal attempts at stopping rapid price increases were required, but efforts did not help.

Reaganomics/Trickle-Down Supply-Side/Devolution New Federalism
R. Reagan
Early 1980s
The goals were to cut federal programs and business regulations. Tax cuts in the name of expansion were central.

Monetary policy: When the economy is in recession, government should lower interest rates and buy bonds from the public. When there is too much inflation, the Federal Reserve should raise interest rates and sell bonds to the public, lowering the supply of money.

"Trickle-down" policies: This term gained popularity in the 1980s when it described the effort to cut government control of business and emphasized the need to help businesses create more wealth. This wealth would "trickle" through all of the economy. Opponents of this policy used the term "voodoo economics," as during primary campaigning by candidate George H. W. Bush while he was still running against Ronald Reagan.

Federal Mandates and the Budget

Many recent forms of federal assistance have come with "strings attached"—rules that must be followed by states that use the money. Highway funds of the past were controlled by speed limit and driving age rules. Education funds have recently been connected to testing requirements.

When the federal government creates programs without supporting funds, known as unfunded mandates, states can balk at those programs. Recent suits by local governments over unfunded gun control rules were won by states, and the rules did not have to be followed. When states need money for important social programs, however, they must follow national guidelines.

❯❯ II. DOMESTIC POLICY DEVELOPMENT

Introduction

National domestic policy priorities have become more elaborate, and the scope of federal involvement in public policy has grown in recent times. Debates will certainly continue about the effectiveness of government in trying to solve social problems or economic ills. Some reforms, such as the creation of the Securities and Exchange Commission (SEC), which regulates the stock market, and the Food and Drug Administration (FDA), which ensures that harmful foods and medicines are not available to the population, are supported by most citizens.

Kinds of Policies

Policies of the U.S. government fall into three basic categories. The first category encompasses *distributive policies.* Distributive policies are aimed at specific groups and are very selective in nature. Farm and industrial subsidies provide billions to companies that grow critical food supplies or build important products. Prescription drug companies, energy providers, and the airline industry all benefit from government subsidy programs. These programs are also popular with political leaders, as they tend to create voter support among the employees of such companies, while also garnering generous campaign contributions from the corporations themselves.

Regulatory policies are aimed at changing behaviors, such as criminal activities or alcohol and tobacco use. Clean water and air policies might also be used to force industries to reduce the amount of pollutants they produce. The Environmental Protection Agency (EPA) regulates the amount of pollutants that can be released into the air and water. The SEC is a regulatory commission that oversees the stock market as well as other financial exchanges. The SEC was initially created to prevent another depression; however, its modern role also includes investigating corporate corruption, such as the Enron scandal, and fraud, such as Bernie Madoff's Ponzi scheme in 2008.

Redistributive policies are aimed at giving financial assistance to those who are seen as needing it. Redistributive programs originated during the Great Depression and have become a source of controversy in recent years. Public opinion remains divided on whether or not entitlement programs should continue in their present form or if they should be substantially reduced.

Grant Programs

The system of federal grants continues to be a source of controversy with regard to policy and funding. Congress can grant states money for programs that the states control but require certain federal rules be followed. States often chafe under federal rules but are stuck with following them or losing needed federal funds. One example of this practice is how the federal government regulates highway speed limits, although that power was officially left up to the states. A 1973 law prohibited federal highway grants for states with interstate speed limits set higher than 55 mph. The law was repealed in 1995, but for more than 20 years, the federal government was able to regulate the speed limit on a national level. A more modern example of federal grant regulation can be seen in our public education system. The No Child Left Behind program, which was created under the administration of President George W. Bush, emphasizes the accountability of schools in state-run public education systems. However, this program has been accused of being an unfunded mandate. This means that the government has created stricter federal requirements but has not allotted any federal funding to help the schools adhere to the new requirements. The Americans with Disabilities Act, which requires nearly all private businesses to be accessible to the disabled but does not assist business owners with the cost of conforming to the act, is another example of an unfunded mandate.

The Basics Of Policy Development

Agenda setting. What are the priorities? What is important to the voting population? Congress often listens to public opinion as a cue to what issues should be addressed. Polls and media reports often influence perceptions of what issues appear to be most important.

Policy formation: How can government attack the problem? Proposed actions require studies of potential costs, logistical requirements, long- and short-term effects on the affected parties, and other complexities. To create a clearer picture of the effects of a proposed policy, reviewers look at cost-benefit analysis data to compare the probable costs with the projected rewards. If a prohibitively expensive problem exists and the proposed policy would only help a very few, then the issue might be dropped as too costly.

Policy adoption: This is the part of the process that receives the most media attention. A policy is submitted as a bill to Congress. It is debated and revised until it either dies or passes through Congress to the executive branch.

Policy implementation: Someone must apply the new rules of the policy. Depending on the scope of the policy, an agency within the executive branch may be selected. In response to the terrorist attacks of September 11, 2001, a new cabinet position was created to oversee homeland security policies. Independent government agencies, such as the SEC or the EPA, are specialized, not generally implementing policies outside of their specific focuses.

Policy evaluation: The public and the members of government react to the new laws and decide whether or not changes are needed. In theory, if the problem is solved, the government reduces controls, but history shows that agencies rarely go away. They just evolve to perform new forms of monitoring or new kinds of duties.

Major Developments in Domestic Policy

Late 1800s (Gilded Age): The beginnings of policies for workers developed. Major battles occurred over the issue of union rights. European reforms on child labor influenced the United States. The People's (Populist) Party platform of 1892 brought "radical" calls for policy changes. Examples included legal unions, public transportation, civil service reform, a national currency, graduated income taxes, and new national bank controls.

Early 1900s (Progressive Era): The breakup of Standard Oil signaled moves to control excessive business practices, monopolies, and trusts. The Panic of 1907 brought calls for banking reforms and led to the eventual creation of the Federal Reserve System. The collapse of the stock market in 1929 led to calls for controls on insider trading, now monitored by the SEC.

Mid-1930s (New Deal): The executive branch moved to the forefront of economic development and job programs. Social Security was adopted as a major public safety net. WWII military spending created a long-term reliance on military jobs, contracts, bases, and industries.

Late 1900s (Cold War Era, Great Society): Government led the attempts to reduce poverty, support agricultural production through subsidies, control inflation with interest rates, and spur economic growth with reduced taxes. Medicare and Medicaid programs were expanded, and discussions were held concerning changes in medical care. Environmental programs were expanded, protections were added for those with disabilities, and the government moved to increase support of public schools.

Early 2000s: Although the environment has remained a major issue, renewable energy and less reliance on foreign oil have come to the forefront. Universal healthcare has been a major issue since President Obama took office in January 2009.

❯❯ III. FOREIGN POLICY: MILITARY AND ECONOMIC

Introduction

Foreign policy decisions have always been a special power of the executive branch. The need for single and forceful leadership, speedy decisions, and direct negotiations gives presidents control over most interactions with foreign powers. Congress has authority to ratify treaties, but the president's roles as negotiator and commander-in-chief are paramount.

The history of leadership in the government often also details the history of presidents pushing foreign and military initiatives. The vast majority of past military conflicts have occurred because the president ordered troops into dangerous situations that often lasted years. In only five instances has Congress itself actually declared war.

WARS DECLARED BY CONGRESS

- 1812: Against the United Kingdom
- 1846: Against Mexico
- 1898: Against Spain
- 1917: Against Germany, Austro-Hungary, Turkey
- 1941: Against Japan (Germany and Italy declared war on the United States after December 8, 1941.)

MILITARY CONFLICTS WITHOUT DECLARATIONS OF WAR (ALTHOUGH AUTHORIZED BY CONGRESS)

- 1802: Barbary Coast
- 1817: Florida, Spain
- 1845: Mexico (border fight)
- 1918: Russian Civil War
- 1958: Lebanon
- 1962: Vietnam (until 1972)
- 1983: Lebanon
- 1991: Gulf War
- 2001: Afghanistan
- 2002: Iraq

MILITARY ENGAGEMENTS AUTHORIZED BY UNITED NATIONS SECURITY COUNCIL RESOLUTIONS

- 1950: Korea
- 1992: Bosnia

The Rise of "Agreements" Over Treaties

Presidents make executive agreements with foreign leaders that do not require senatorial approval. These agreements are so common in modern times that "treaties" are rarely proposed anymore. In recent years, treaties aimed at the reduction of nuclear weapons have been met with considerable congressional opposition. Preseidential administrations find it much simpler to cut deals at the agreement level and then wait to see if they work. If formal treaties are then needed, they can be negotiated. Moreover, moves to eliminate tariffs across the globe have reduced the need for many economic treaties. The collapse of the Soviet Union has lessened the need for military alliances.

Helping the President

A large bureaucratic system backs the president's agenda. The State Department runs hundreds of embassies with legions of highly trained Foreign Service workers. The U.S. "intelligence community" includes the CIA (Central Intelligence Agency), the NSA (National Security Agency), and lesser-known agencies that provide the president with detailed and secret sets of data. The Defense Department has several strategies at its disposal, including covert operations, political coercion, and military intervention, if diplomacy breaks down.

The Importance of Policy Decisions

Foreign policy decisions can be critical and long lasting. They usually do not involve military attacks. Most policies concern programs of financial assistance through grants, loans, or building projects. The United States also works with the major international organizations—it is the major funding country of the United Nations (UN), hosts its headquarters, and is a permanent member of the governing Security Council. The United States was central in the development of the World Trade Organization (WTO), which takes a leading role in the negotiations covering trade and tariff concerns. The United States also remains a leading member of the North Atlantic Treaty Organization (NATO), the North American Free Trade Agreement (NAFTA), and other international associations. In the summer of 2005, the Congress debated and voted on U.S. involvement concerning the creation of the Central America Free Trade Agreement/Association (CAFTA). In August 2005, President Bush signed the legislation for the Central America-Dominican Republic-United States Free Trade Agreement (CAFTA-DR). On January 1, 2009, the agreement expanded to include Costa Rica, making the agreement complete among all seven participating countries.

Major Leaders in Foreign Policy

President—the role of "chief diplomat"

White House staff and vice president—assist, filter news, and help with decisions

Joint chiefs of staff of the U.S. military services—provide military options and data

Central Intelligence Agency—in charge of gathering information

Ambassadors and staff of the Department of State—keep the leaders informed of the situation overseas and often act as negotiation intermediaries.

National Security Council (President, VP, Secretary of Defense, Secretary of State)— the formal group that meets to formulate policy and actions

Foreign Intelligence Advisory Board—section of the executive office that guides the gathering of information from various intelligence agencies

Assistant to the President for National Security Affairs—the head of many executive teams that specialize in such issues

Council of Economic Advisors (three appointed members)—give advice on tax and other money programs that affect international trade.

National Economic Council—in charge of advising the president on global economic policy

ORGANIZATIONS AFFECTING FOREIGN POLICY

- **CAFTA**—The Central American Free Trade Agreement, enacted in 2005, forms a free trade zone for this region.

- **European Union (EU)**—Although not a member, the United States is greatly affected by the formation of Europe as a large free-trade zone. The currency of the EU, the euro, competes with the dollar for international investments and exchanges. Most members of the EU use the euro, but some (like the United Kingdom) have kept their old currencies. In the summer of 2005, moves to consolidate the union further politically were rejected by France and Denmark. The EU will continue to evolve. As of 2010, Croatia, Iceland, the former Yugoslav Republic of Macedonia, and Turkey are all candidates to join the EU.

- **G-8 "summits"**—These are meetings that are held by leaders of the United States, Great Britain, Russia, China, Germany, France, Japan, and Canada. The meetings are held to further international cooperation and development through the Group of Eight.

- **International Monetary Fund (IMF)**—The United States is a leading member of this organization, which attempts to promote monetary cooperation.

- **NAFTA**—The North American Free Trade Agreement was approved during the Clinton administration and established free trade among the United States, Canada, and Mexico.

- **North Atlantic Treaty Organization (NATO)**—Originally organized to protect Western Europe from communist aggression, NATO has changed and expanded greatly since the collapse of the Soviet Union. NATO now includes former communist countries of Eastern Europe.

- **United Nations (UN)**—The UN attempts to establish world security, political rights, and stability. It has 192 member countries and is headquartered in New York City.

- **World Bank**—This international organization gives loans and subsidies to many countries, especially developing nations.

- **World Trade Organization (WTO)**—Created in the late 1990s, the WTO is an international effort to eliminate tariffs, expand free trade, and protect international laws concerning copyright and intellectual property.

Practice Section

1. The Congressional Budget Office carries out which of the following responsibilities?

   (A) It consists of a professional staff accountable for giving Congress budget projections and balancing the Office of Management and Budget priorities.

   (B) It consists of senators and representatives who keep an eye on committee spending.

   (C) It consists of members of the executive and legislative branches who manage congressional spending.

   (D) It is made up of congressional assistants who oversee the expenses of their superiors.

   (E) It consists of members of the State Department who are expected to limit congressional spending.

2. The Fair Deal economic agenda was named and created by which of the following presidents?

   (A) Lyndon Johnson

   (B) John Kennedy

   (C) Franklin Roosevelt

   (D) Ronald Reagan

   (E) Harry Truman

3. Which of the following statements regarding economic policies is NOT correct?

   (A) The phrase *inflation* refers to general rising prices in the economy as a result of extreme consumer demand or spikes in the costs of producing goods.

   (B) Discretionary spending deals with programs that Congress can choose whether or not to fund.

   (C) A flat tax is a tax rate that rises the more income one earns.

   (D) The term *fiscal year* for the federal government refers to the period from October 1 to September 30.

   (E) Mandatory spending refers to budget items Congress is obligated to support.

4. The term *New Federalism* relates to which of the following?

   (A) The increasing influence of iron triangles on the federal budget

   (B) The rising control of the federal government over local and municipal governments

   (C) More government spending for public education

   (D) The conservative movement's goal of returning more control of funds to state authorities

   (E) The economic policy of removing the graduated income tax and replacing it with other forms of governmental revenue

5. Legislation employed by members of Congress to earn favors for home constituents and to pad a congressperson's voting support from local constituents is referred to as

   (A) ex post facto legislation.

   (B) discretionary legislation.

   (C) de jure legislation.

   (D) de facto legislation.

   (E) pork barrel legislation.

6. Which kind of grants demands competitive bids and often also requires some matching money?

   (A) Grants-in-aid

   (B) Project grants

   (C) Formula grants

   (D) Block grants

   (E) None of the above

7. In which domestic policy era was the idea of Social Security accepted as a major public safety net?

   (A) Gilded Age

   (B) Cold War

   (C) Great Society

   (D) Progressive Era

   (E) New Deal

8. When programs for assistance call for recipients to show the government evidence of need, usually determined by low income levels, they are utilizing which of the following concepts?

   (A) Block grants

   (B) Cost-benefit analysis

   (C) Means testing

   (D) Earned income tax credits

   (E) Workfare policies

9. Which of the following statements explains the dynamic of "unfunded mandates"?

   (A) The federal government passes laws without assigning specific funds to execute the changes.

   (B) The federal government passes a law that necessitates no spending on a state's part.

   (C) The federal government merely proposes that states follow certain policies.

   (D) The state government passes laws that involve certain actions on the federal government's part.

   (E) None of the above statements relate to the process of "unfunded mandates."

10. Which of the following is the international organization that provides loans and subsidies to developing nations?

    (A) EEU

    (B) UNICEF

    (C) World Health Organization

    (D) World Bank

    (E) World Trade Organization

11. Which statement best defines the idea of bilateral agreements?

    (A) This kind of agreement relates only to the issue of military bases in the Pacific basin.

    (B) This type of agreement is between two nations with the purpose of creating joint policies.

    (C) This type of agreement deals with offensive-type weapons only.

    (D) This type of agreement is concerned only with missile deployment.

    (E) None of the above definitions describe the concept of bilateral agreements.

12. Which of the following statements regarding the European Union (EU) is accurate?

    (A) The United Kingdom chose to retain its old currency, despite becoming a member of the EU.

    (B) While the United States is not a member of the EU, it is greatly influenced by the policies of the EU.

    (C) Croatia and Turkey are candidates to join the EU.

    (D) The official currency of the EU is called the euro.

    (E) All of the above statements are true concerning the EU.

13. Which of the following sentences is NOT accurate regarding foreign policy and the military?

    (A) The majority of military conflicts in which the United States has been involved have not resulted in a declaration of war by Congress.

    (B) Presidents declare "executive agreements" with foreign countries that do not require senatorial consent.

    (C) Foreign policy decisions are important and lasting and generally do not require military attacks.

    (D) The Defense Department controls hundreds of embassies with a multitude of highly trained Foreign Service workers.

    (E) There is a sizeable bureaucratic system supporting the president's foreign policy plan.

Answers and Explanations

1. A

The Congressional Budget Office is composed of professionals in charge of giving Congress budget projections, among other things.

2. E

President Harry Truman referred to his economic program as the "Fair Deal." Choice (A) is wrong because President Lyndon Johnson called his economic program the "Great Society." Choice (B) is incorrect because John Kennedy's program was named the "New Frontier." Choice (C) is incorrect because Franklin Roosevelt's economic program was referred to as the "New Deal," and choice (D) is incorrect since Ronald Reagan's program was named "Reaganomics."

3. C

With the flat tax, the tax rate does not increase the more one earns. Instead, the flat tax applies the same tax rate regardless of the total income earned. Under a graduated tax, the rate escalates as income increases.

4. D

The phrase *New Federalism* refers to the conservative movement hoping to return more authority and control of money to the states.

5. E

Pork barrel legislation is used by Congress to earn favors for home constituents. It is one of many reasons that defeating an incumbent is easier said than done.

6. B

Project grants demand competitive bids, and they also often require matching funds.

7. E

Social Security was accepted as a public safety net during the New Deal period. It started as a program to help the elderly and to stimulate economic activity during the Great Depression. It was a part of the New Deal under FDR.

8. C

When programs for assistance call for recipients to show evidence of financial need (usually a low income level), they are employing means testing.

9. A

Unfunded mandates happen when the federal government passes laws without allocating exact funds that local and state governments can use to execute the changes.

10. D

The World Bank specializes in providing loans and subsidies to many countries, especially developing nations.

11. B

Bilateral agreements are agreements between two nations for the purpose of creating joint policies. This is in contrast to unilateral policies, wherein a single country declares changes in domestic or foreign policies.

12. E

All of the statements listed are accurate concerning the European Union: The United Kingdom decided to keep its old currency although it is a member of the EU; although the United States is not a member of the EU, it is greatly affected by formation of the EU; Croatia and Turkey are candidates to join the EU; and the official currency of the EU is the euro.

13. D

It is not the Defense Department that runs the hundreds of United States embassies throughout the world. That responsibility belongs to the State Department.

Glossary

advice and consent The power of Congress to confirm or deny presidential nominations for executive and judicial posts and approve of international treaties.

affirmative action Government and private policies designed to provide equal opportunity for minority groups that have suffered from discrimination in the past. Recent challenges have been based on the idea that affirmative action creates reverse discrimination against majority-group citizens.

Aid to Families with Dependent Children (AFDC) The main form of individual welfare payments until the mid-1990s. More recent programs come in the form of grants to states, where the state distributes the family assistance as needed.

American Bar Association (ABA) The organization that ranks federal judicial nominees as well qualified, qualified, or not qualified. These rankings are used to assess nominees prior to their hearings in the Senate.

amicus curiae brief Summary case arguments given by interested parties who may be affected by the outcome of a case. This "friend of the court" summary is supposed to give judges more information about the arguments and the possible outcomes.

balanced budget The goal of the federal government to spend only the amount of money collected from tax revenues.

ballot initiative A form of direct democracy that allows citizens to petition for issues that will be decided by a direct ballot and not by the legislative branch.

bicameral Having or consisting of two legislative chambers or houses, such as Congress being comprised of the House of Representatives and the Senate.

bilateral agreement The resulting agreement when two nations create a joint policy.

block grants Monies given to communities and states for general programs, such as social services and development projects.

budget resolution A congressional resolution binding the legislature to a specific total budget amount for the fiscal year.

categorical grants Grants given to communities and states for very specific programs that require certain conditions or rules to be applied by the agencies spending the federal monies.

caucus A meeting of leaders of a political party to select candidates. Congressional caucuses are used to develop strategies and conduct party business.

charter school programs Primary or secondary schools that receive public money but do not have to adhere to some of the rules and regulations that apply to other public schools in exchange for some type of accountability for producing certain results.

checks and balances The system that allows each of the three branches of government to "check" the power of the other two and limit that power, if necessary, to maintain balance.

clear and present danger test The policy limiting the rights of free speech if the government deems certain forms of speech as a clear and present danger to the public. These limits were first defined in the case *Schenk v. United States,* 1919.

client politics Policies developed to help specific, smaller groups, where the costs of the actions will be borne by the nation as a whole.

closed primary system The regulation that voters must preregister with a party to cast ballots on primary day, or the system where voters can vote in only one party's primary.

closed rule A procedure used by the House of Representatives to prohibit amendments from being offered in order to speed consideration of the bill.

cloture Procedure developed in the Senate to end filibuster through votes. The rules for cloture are based on approval of 60 senators. If cloture passes against a filibuster, those delaying must end their actions within a set amount of time and allow business to move forward.

Code of Federal Regulations (CFR) A series of volumes comprising a list of rules for the various departments and bureaucracies.

Commerce Clause Article 1, Section 8, Clause 3 gives Congress the power to "regulate Commerce with Foreign Nations, and among the several States...."

commercial speech A form of speech regulated and restricted to uphold "truth in advertising." Deception for the sake of monetary gains is not legal. The Federal Trade Commission (FTC) is in charge of such regulations.

concurring opinion A document drafted by court justices who voted with the majority to explain how they differ in their beliefs about the meaning of the majority vote.

"consent of the governed" Describes a government that derives its power from the governed and does not force its power on the citizens.

constant campaign The manner in which members of the House, who must face re-election every other year, and presidential candidates continually campaign to the public to uphold their positions.

constituent Voters from the district or state that elected that leader. House members' constituents are from their districts. Senators' constituents are from the entire state.

continuing resolution An action allowing government agencies to continue to be funded temporarily if Congress is unable to complete the new federal budget by the October 1 deadline.

continuous body The Senate is a continuous body in that only one-third of the Senate is up for re-election at a time. All of the House is up for re-election every other year and all seats could be changed. Therefore, the House is not "continuous."

debt/public debt The combined deficits of the federal government owed in the form of bonds sold to U.S. citizens, foreign investors, countries, and parts of government. In mid-2010, the total debt came to about $13.4 trillion.

de facto segregation Racial or ethnic separation that exists without the support of laws or political action.

de jure segregation A form of discrimination that occurs when laws segregate citizens based on religion, ethnicity, or other grounds.

discharge petition A process in the House that can allow some bills to be released from committee without committee approval.

discretionary spending The programs that Congress can choose to fund. Even though spending to run the government and maintaining the military are seen as given needs, such funding is considered discretionary due to possible changes in the level of funding.

Earned Income Tax Credit Credits calculated by the Internal Revenue Service to provide financial assistance to low-income workers that can be paid at tax time in April.

Elastic Clause Article 1, Section 8, Clause 18: Congress's power "To make all Laws which shall be necessary and proper..." is a basis of Congress adapting to the needs of the times.

electoral college The process by which electors are selected by states and are "directed" by the popular vote to select the president.

entitlement A payment required by law that is given to people who meet certain eligibility requirements, such as Social Security payments.

environmental impact study A study showing the possible adverse effects of work by government agencies or private industry receiving government assistance on the air, land, or water. The study is then given public review, and decisions are made as to whether or not the damage can be avoided, repaired, or ignored.

Establishment Clause A law based on the First Amendment's section about the status of religion. "Congress shall make no law respecting an establishment of religion...." Government cannot lead citizens in the practices of certain religions, giving preference to those religions.

exclusionary rule The idea that evidence obtained in some illegal manner cannot be used in court against the defendant.

ex post facto A law barring government agencies from inflicting punishment for events that occurred when something was legal but has since been made illegal.

fast-track authority Pieces of legislation that must be voted on "as is" without amendment attempts. Presidents are sometimes given this authority when beginning talks concerning treaties so that the Senate must take or leave them.

Federalist Papers A collection of essays by the Federalists that advocated for the ratification of the Constitution.

Federal Register The official publication of the federal government that contains most routine publications and public notices of government agencies.

filibuster A strategy used in the Senate to speak a bill to death by delaying votes, stopping other legislation, etc., until the bill sponsors give up.

fiscal year Refers to the federal budget year (October 1 to September 30).

flat tax A national tax level that would be figured at a fixed rate.

Freedom of Information Act A 1966 law created by Congress to help ensure that agencies are acting in the most open manner available and citizens can petition to see files of agencies.

General Schedule Rating (GS Rating) The salaries of members of the civil service are set in levels, ranging from GS1 to GS18, eliminating pay disparities in different parts of government.

gerrymandering The division of voting districts with the goal of guaranteeing seats for one party.

graduated income tax The progressive ideal that people with higher levels of income should pay higher percentages of tax.

Great Compromise (Connecticut Plan, Sherman Plan) An agreement between large and small states reached during the Constitutional Convention that defined the legislative structure and representation that each state would have under the United States Constitution. It created a bicameral legislature, in which each state has equal representation in the Senate and representation in the House of Representatives is based on a state's population.

hold A request for a delay in the discussion of a bill in the Senate. If the leadership agrees, this hold can be a permanent block to the bill.

House Un-American Activities Committee The investigative committee that gained notoriety during the Cold War for its hunts of communists in the United States.

impeach The act of charging a public official (often the president) with criminal acts or misconduct while in office. The House can impeach, and the Senate must decide whether to remove a person as a result of an impeachment.

incorporation The ability of the Bill of Rights to be applied to state governments through the requirements of the 14th Amendment.

incumbent A person already holding an office, often seeking re-election.

inflation The rise in the general level of prices of goods and services in an economy over a period of time. Inflation is caused by excessive consumer demand or spikes in the costs of producing goods.

informal amendments An adjustment to one of the amendments to the Constitution without formally passing the change.

interest group People who support a cause and work together for political interests.

interest payments on the debt The payments required each budget year for the owed interest on the public debt of the United States.

Jim Crow laws The various laws and practices of segregation, primarily in the South, installed after Reconstruction ended in 1876–1877.

judicial review The power of the Supreme Court to evaluate the constitutional status of laws and lower court rulings, established as a result of the case *Marbury v. Madison*, 1803.

Lemon Test A test for the level of financial involvement of government agencies in religious schools based on *Lemon v. Kurtzman*, 1971. The government may assist religious entities if (1) there is a legitimate secular purpose for the help, (2) the help does not have the primary effect of advancing or prohibiting religion, and (3) the help does not create "excessive entanglement" between the government and the religion.

litmus test Issues such as abortion, gay rights, and gun control that are important enough to determine where voters will give their support or how certain elected officials will vote.

majority opinion The decision written by justices of the Supreme Court describing why they made a specific ruling.

mandatory spending Budget items that Congress is required to fund.

midterm elections The elections for all members of the House of Representatives and one-third of the senators held when the presidency is not up for election.

Miranda warning An advisement of one's rights that must take place before police can question someone they have arrested.

New Federalism A conservative movement designed to return more power and control of money to the states. The term was coined during the Nixon presidency.

New Hampshire primary Traditionally, these are the first of the public votes in the new presidential election. In 2008, it was held January 8.

New Jersey Plan (Paterson Plan) The smaller states' counter to the Virginia Plan. It proposed a unicameral (one chamber) Congress with equal representation for all states.

original jurisdiction A court's authority to hear and decide a case for the first time.

patronage (or the "spoils system") The act of doling out political positions to supporters of a party and its candidates, often used as incentive to gain that support. The system was so corrupt that major reforms now limit such appointments to very few positions.

penumbra rights Rights not clearly defined but existing in the "shadow" of formal constitutional rights.

An example would be privacy rights in the shadow of First Amendment.

per curium **decisions** Legal decisions that are made anonymously.

Plum Book The list of federal positions, published by Congress, that are open to presidential appointments. The list includes about 400 upper policy-making positions and 2,500 positions all together.

pork/pork-barrel ("earmarks") Legislation that is often local and intended to help districts with contracts and money. These are used by members of Congress to gain favors from home constituents and pad voting support.

quorum The number of members of a group needed to hold an official meeting or conduct binding votes. The traditional number in the U.S. Congress is half of members plus one.

realignment The major regrouping of support within political parties. The New Deal was a source of realignment for Democrats, and the Reagan election did the same for Republicans.

reapportionment The periodic redistribution of U.S. congressional seats according to changes in the census figures.

recess appointments The ability of the president to fill vacant federal positions, such as federal court judgeships, without senatorial approval if the Senate is in recess.

reciprocity The pattern of collecting vote promises from other members of Congress in exchange for vote support for their bills and projects.

revolving door The practice of major lobby groups hiring recently retired members of Congress for high-paying positions. The advantage of having a person who knows all the secret maneuvers of policy, has long experience with the key power brokers, and has made lasting friendships with those creating laws is seen as a major, and sneaky, advantage for those lobby groups with large amounts of money for such salaries.

rider An amendment, usually not of national import, attached to a larger and more important bill to allow the amendment to pass more easily.

safe seat A term used when a representative appears to have an overwhelming level of local support in the home district. With greater uses of gerrymandering to ensure party domination, safe seats have become more common.

school voucher programs The reform initiative by conservative groups to reallocate tax funds normally given to large school systems to parents in the form of refunds. This tax voucher allows parents to use the money to send their children to private schools. Recent challenges to such programs have focused on the use of public tax dollars to enrich church-run schools. In 2002, the Supreme Court held in the case of *Zelman v. Simmons-Harris* that some vouchers could be used for private schools.

shield laws Laws passed by states giving the press protection from revealing sources.

split-ticket voting A trend where voters select different candidates of different parties for various offices from the same long ballot. These are more independent voters.

social contract The concept that people will follow the rules established by their government in exchange for order and safety.

stare decisis The practice of basing legal decisions on Supreme Court precedents from similar cases.

straight-ticket voting The practice of voting for candidates of the same party for multiple positions.

Strategic Arms Limitations Talks treaties (SALT treaties) A set of agreements that began the process of reducing the number of missile and nuclear weapons.

Strategic Defense Initiative (SDI) or "Star Wars weapons" The Reagan administration program to place antimissile weapons in space.

street-level (bureaucrats) The government employees who work directly with the public in the implementation of federal and local programs.

subsidies Money assistance given to farmers and businesses aimed at protecting against monopolies, helping struggling companies, and providing sufficient resources for future growth.

summit diplomacy A series of efforts made in the Cold War period to have the leaders of major powers sit down together and work on issues and conflicts.

superdelegates The members of Congress and members of the national committee given a certain set of votes at the Democratic National Convention. These delegates were created as part of Democratic Party reforms of the 1970s.

Superfund The name for the Comprehensive Environmental Response, Compensation, and Liability Act of 1980 (CERCLA), a federal law designed to clean up sites contaminated with hazardous waste.

supermajority A requirement for a proposed piece of legislation to gain a specified level of support which exceeds a simple majority (over 50%).

surplus The amount of money left over in the budget when the government spends less than it collects in taxes. Rapid economic expansions of incomes created brief surpluses in the late 1990s, but these were eliminated by the crisis of 9/11, the recession of late 2001, tax cuts of 2001 and 2002, and the conflicts in Afghanistan and Iraq.

transfer payment A payment that transfers wealth from higher to lower income individuals. These payments are made to individuals by the federal government through various social benefit programs.

unilateral policies A term defining the efforts of a single country to change policies and align those changes with their relations with other countries.

Virginia Plan (Randolph Plan, Madison Plan) An outline of a constitution drafted by Madison before the formal meetings began. It proposed a bicameral legislature (two chambers) but gave populated states the most representation in both houses. The general outline was used by the convention delegates to build the basic framework of the Constitution, thus giving Madison the nickname "Father of the Constitution."

war chest The amount of money a candidate has created for the next campaign. This is usually a tremendous advantage for incumbents.

whip A traditional name of the assistant to the House majority and minority leaders.

workfare A reform initiative of the welfare system to require recipients to find employment in order to receive governmental assistance.

writ of mandamus The power given to federal courts to require action by citizens or governmental agencies.

writ of habeas corpus A court order that requires a judge to evaluate whether there is sufficient cause for keeping a person in jail.

yellow journalism A late-1800s trend of sensationalist news that helped influence government policy. The best example is the Hearst papers, which helped create the Spanish-American War crisis.

Index